BATTLE
RHYTHM

PRAYING IN SYNC WITH GOD'S HEART

JAMAAL BERNARD

Battle Rhythm:
Praying in Sync with God's Heart
Jamaal Bernard

ISBN 979-8-218-12755-8

First Edition

1 2 3 4 5 6   25 24 23 22

FORWARD
BY A. R. BERNARD

One of the mentors in my life, Jim Rhon, said, "Life is a fight for territory. Whenever you stop fighting for what you want, what you don't want will take the territory."

The result of Adam and Eve's fall in the Garden of Eden was the toil of everyday life. *Toil* means, "long, strenuous, fatiguing labor." The world that was designed by God to cooperate with human flourishing is now antagonistic. Life became both threat and promise. Adversity with opportunity. Opportunity with opposition.

God's mandate in Genesis 1:28, to "Be fruitful and multiply," is still in effect but under different conditions — conditions that require a different approach.

We all know that your attitude determines how you approach life. Attitude is having the right frame of mind, the right intellectual and emotional disposition. How you approach life will determine success or failure.

In his book, "Battle Rhythm," my son, Jamaal Bernard, takes on the job of shaping your mindset with the right attitude for success in life. In this 90-day devotional, each day is filled with Godly wisdom and inspiration to face the battle of life.

Jamaal reminds us that we never face life alone. God promised to be with us each step of the way. He makes His wisdom and favor available to those who are willing to let Him walk with them through the highs and lows of life. But we have the responsibility to develop the way we think and the way we approach life. We are responsible for developing a winning attitude.

In the book of 3rd John, verse 2, we have a greeting from the Apostle John to someone named Gaius. Some scholars would like to reduce it to a simple greeting. But it is part of God's inspired Word, expressing the original intent in the mind of God for humanity.

"Beloved, I wish above all things, that you prosper and be in health, even as your soul prospers." (3rd John 2, KJV)

With these words, I encourage you to begin this 90-day devotional journey to a winning mindset and a better life.

— A.R. Bernard

What then shall we say to these things? If

God is for us, who can be against us?

— Romans 8:31

Believing in God for the Victory

And we also thank God constantly for this, that when you received the word of God, which you heard from us, you accepted it not as the word of men but as what it really is, the word of God, which is at work in you believers.
— 1 Thessalonians 2:13

A re you living like an overcomer? It is time to believe the Word at work in you and shift fright to fearlessness! Your thoughts, posture, and choices will move in concert with God attracting the victory in your life. The anonymous woman in Mark, chapter five must have felt hopeless after doctors had failed to cure her of the painful hemorrhaging she had suffered for twelve years (Mark 5:25). Society marked her as legally unclean, banning her from community gatherings; approaching Jesus would have been out of the question. Her pain didn't pause her passion, and she refused to allow fear, doubt, or shame to hold her back from touching the hem of His garment. One person's belief—one bold move, and she was healed. When you reach out by faith in God, boldly coming before the Lord, you will find healing— physical, emotional, mental, and financial. Today, trust that God is working everything out for your good and declare, "I have the victory!"

Lord, I pray that You continue to guide, guard, and govern my steps. Keep me in Your will and show me Your way.

_____

_____

_____

_____

_____

_____

_____

_____

_____

_____

_____

_____

_____

_____

_____

_____

_____

_____

_____

Winning Mindset

"For who has understood the mind of the Lord so as to instruct him?" But we have the mind of Christ.
— 1 Corinthians 2:16

Having the mind of Christ is to have a winning mindset. There are negative influences around us competing for our attention. Television, social media, and the people we spend time with contribute to the cynicism that tries to discourage us. Jesus knew the manipulative whispers of Satan, the tempter. Our Lord can relate to being face to face with the enemy. Our challenge today is to do what Christ did. He did not retreat. His sword and shield were the Word of His Father. We must constantly communicate with our Heavenly Father, as Christ did. Jesus prayed without ceasing, and we can do the same. There is one place to find help, wisdom, and direction. We are victors, not victims; we are more than conquerors! We can do all things when we intentionally focus our minds on the Lord, not the negativity of this world. Are you ready to shift your focus? You are courageous, victorious, and filled with God's love and grace because your mind is on Him.

Lord, Today I surrender my doubts and fears and put my faith and trust in You. I will seek You before making decisions and will wait to hear Your voice.

_____

_____

_____

_____

_____

_____

_____

_____

_____

_____

_____

_____

_____

_____

_____

_____

_____

_____

_____

_____

_____

FULLY LOADED

*For we do not wrestle against flesh and blood, but against
the rulers, against the authorities, against the cosmic powers
over this present darkness, against the spiritual forces of evil
in the heavenly places.*
— EPHESIANS 6:12

As believers in Christ, we are no longer at the enemy's
mercy. We are more than conquerors in Christ. Living
in a world of constant spiritual warfare, we can go boldly
into every situation, knowing we have every weapon to
defeat the enemy. When we put our faith and trust in the
Lord, we confidently go into battle with our spiritual
ammunition, fully loaded with one in the chamber. The
Word, our prayers, fellowship, fasting, and worship prepare
us for the frontlines. When our ammunition runs low, we
can refill our faith by spending time in the presence of the
Lord. When we are lacking in communion with the Father,
we find ourselves feeling defeated and disconnected. Do you
know that feeling? If you are battle-worn and weary, enter
into the presence of God. Take full advantage of His wisdom,
direction, protection, and correction. Position yourself at all
times, strong, locked, and loaded through the power of the
Holy Spirit, and trust in God in every challenge.

Lord, When I feel empty, I will seek after You. I want to be filled with Your presence and hear Your voice. I will attack the day knowing that You are my strength and shield.

_____
_____
_____
_____
_____
_____
_____
_____
_____
_____
_____
_____
_____
_____
_____
_____
_____
_____
_____
_____
_____
_____

STRATEGIC

Therefore, we are ambassadors for Christ, God making his appeal through us. We implore you on behalf of Christ, be reconciled to God.
— 2 CORINTHIANS 5:20

As Christians, we must choose to be strategic in our faith. More than ever, we need a plan of action to face the dilemmas of the day. God's Word shows us His way, and His Spirit reveals the enemy's schemes in our experience. Do you know the enemy's tricks? By understanding how the enemy operates, you can avoid the traps and temptations he sets. Be sensitive to the subtle, seemingly insignificant cracks he leaves in your path. One careless move, and you're going down. The more knowledge you have about the enemy, the better you can strategize a defense. One of the most vital strategies you can implement is to avoid the same areas of influence that can trip up someone in addiction — people, places, and things. Satan knows exactly which buttons to press, so it is essential to give him no access to your buttons. He can blow a hole in the wall of your resolve with the key you provide him through unhealthy relationships, questionable places, and things that pull your focus from righteous living. Your battle plan must include offensive and defensive strategies through putting on the whole armor of God described in Ephesians 6:10-18: The Helmet of Salvation, Belt of Truth, Breastplate of Righteousness, Shield of Faith, Sword of the Spirit (Word of God), and the Shoes of Readiness. Rejoice that you have an excellent strategy to overcome any difficulty, doubt, or disappointment.

Lord, Thank You for Your Holy Spirit, who heightens my senses and readies me to advance the Gospel and defend against the attacks of the enemy.

_____
_____
_____
_____
_____
_____
_____
_____
_____
_____
_____
_____
_____
_____
_____
_____
_____
_____
_____
_____
_____
_____
_____
_____

FINDING YOUR RHYTHM

For I know the plans I have for you, declares the LORD, plans for welfare and not for evil, to give you a future and a hope.
— JEREMIAH 29:11

In what ways does your spiritual life reflect the strength of your prayer life? It can be tempting to mimic the steps of others to grow in the Lord; however, there is a rhythm of prayer that is all your own, a cadence of communication that fits your shoes perfectly. Rhythm is defined as "a strong, regular, repeated pattern of movement or sound." When you talk with the Lord and walk with Him, you will begin to sense His direction and feel His comfort. His purpose for your life is unique and individual. Do not allow your calling to get lost in comparisons. The same God that provides for others will deliver on His promise to you. He will heal and guide you according to His specific plan for you. Your spiritual battle rhythm is a beat in sync with God's heartbeat, in step with the Holy Spirit. Comfort and peace is knowing that when you walk with the Lord, fixed on His voice, you will not be lost. The Holy Spirit's nudge guides you to redirect your steps to make better decisions. Praise God this day that the Lord has great plans for your life and your family. Seek Him. Allow Him to guide you. Depend on God's revelation as you walk with Him daily, and you will see the future and hope you have in His love.

Lord, Help me see with my spiritual eyes more than my physical eyes. Let my heart be in tune with the pulse of Your heartbeat.

_____

_____

_____

_____

_____

_____

_____

_____

_____

_____

_____

_____

_____

_____

_____

_____

_____

_____

_____

The Call

But now thus says the LORD, he who created you, O Jacob, he who formed you, O Israel: "Fear not, for I have redeemed you; I have called you by name, you are mine."
— Isaiah **43:1**

God has called and uniquely equipped each of us with gifts, talents, skills, and abilities for the growth of the Kingdom. Do you believe you have been called? Are you ready to fully answer the appointment on your life? Many spend their better days fighting against God's plan, often because it comes through unexpected, uncomfortable steps. Look at the story of Jonah: God called Jonah to a place he did not want to go. The farther he ran, the more trouble he found. Jonah landed in some unflattering situations and unpleasant places — like a whale's belly. Today, I challenge you to be intentional about following God's instructions. Often, like Jonah, we want God to use us, but then we want to dictate how He does it. Following God's call on your life requires sacrifice and faith; it demands stepping outside your comfort zone. If you feel like you keep running into dead ends, maybe it's time to reevaluate your position. Are you avoiding following through on a direction God has given you? Will you respond to the call today? Whatever God calls on you to do, trust that He will make room for you and provide everything you need to pursue the call. All He needs is a heart that is willing.

Lord, I surrender my will, my gifts, and my talents that You have given me. Help me to put aside my preferences to accomplish Your purpose. Use me for Your glory.

Driving Force

Do not be slothful in zeal,
be fervent in spirit, serve the Lord.
— Romans 12:11

When you think of the word *force*, what comes to mind? Maybe you think of influence or power, perhaps military strength. Force "implies the actual effective exercise of power." What is the motivating influence on your daily schedule? What thoughts and activities spark your energy and focus? Your values are your driving force, and you cannot allow distractions to disconnect you from your power source. Life is hectic and noisy. It's understandable for any of us to spill energy into the pursuit of things that are unproductive or wasteful, or simply not God's best. I have seen people with incredible ambition and talent, but without God in the driver's seat, they end up dissatisfied. Remember Who you work for when you find yourself depleted of power and passion. The God of the universe desires you to experience incredible miracles, strength, abundance, and fulfillment with His love as the force behind every endeavor. Protect your energy, and you will build a driving force like a fire swelling in your heart, unwavering and unbeatable (Jeremiah 20:9). As Christians, that's the type of driving force we want and need today.

Lord, Help me keep the fire burning in my heart. Be the driving force that guides and directs my footsteps.

_____

_____

_____

_____

_____

_____

_____

_____

_____

_____

_____

_____

_____

_____

_____

_____

_____

_____

In Step with God

If we live by the Spirit,
let us also keep in step with the Spirit.
— Galatians 5:25

There is a barrage of people and influences pulling us this way and that. We question if we are making the right choices. Some of us desire to be people-pleasers, pressured internally to satisfy others, often at our own expense. There seems to be a constant internal battle of wills — we have our preferences and experiences, and others want their say in our decisions, but God's last word must come first. If you have found yourself exhausted, empty, resentful, and confused about your value, get in the presence of the Lord and resync with how He sees you and why He created you. It is a remarkable thing when you find your peace and fulfillment in step with God, knowing you are where you are supposed to be — right place, right time, right you. You will never access your blessing marching to someone else's beat. Seek God's will for your life and find yourself in step with Him, to enjoy a consistent, abundant life of peace, joy, and love.

Lord, Let me be in continual alignment with Your will. Show me when I am losing my way and bring me back in alignment with Your heart.

_____

_____

_____

_____

_____

_____

_____

_____

_____

_____

_____

_____

_____

_____

_____

_____

_____

_____

_____

_____

REGROUP

Finally, brothers, whatever is true, whatever is honorable, whatever is just, whatever is pure, whatever is lovely, whatever is commendable, if there is any excellence, if there is anything worthy of praise, think about these things.
— PHILIPPIANS 4:8

Maybe you are reading this devotion today and feel like you are hanging on by a thread in a hurricane. When you are frazzled and feel spun round, you need to slow down, take a deep breath, and regroup. To regroup is "to organize something again in order to make a new effort, especially after a defeat." No one said the Christian life would be easy, but we have the assurance that when times get tough, we are not alone. Our Father is there to pick us up and calm us so we can regroup and continue — or reassess and adopt a new strategy. When the feelings of unraveling begin, the primary suspect is the mind. Prayerfully and purposefully organize your perceptions. I encourage you to restructure your attention around gratitude and redirect your focus on God's will for your life. Remember, no matter what you may be dealing with, God's plans for your life are still to prosper you and give you a bright future.

Lord, Balance my thinking. Keep my mind plumb and level through Your Word and Your Spirit.

_____
_____
_____
_____
_____
_____
_____
_____
_____
_____
_____
_____
_____
_____
_____
_____
_____
_____
_____
_____
_____
_____

On Track

Do not swerve to the right or to the left;
turn your foot away from evil.
— Proverbs 4:27

Have you ever gotten distracted while driving and missed your exit? In life, as in traveling, sometimes we journey quite a distance in the wrong direction before realizing we're lost. With the busyness of living, we can so easily get sidetracked. Today, I want to encourage you to get back on course.

Firstly, pull over. Evaluate where you are and make the corrective turns necessary to right your route.

Secondly, ask for directions. Humble yourself and accept help from God and whomever He sends your way.

And lastly, keep your eyes on the road. Do not allow your attention to be drawn from the path. Stay centered on the Lord and His direction to get back on track and stay on track.

Lord, Give me the strength to stay on track no matter the obstacles or detours I might face. Help me to focus and keep my paths straight.

_____

_____

_____

_____

_____

_____

_____

_____

_____

_____

_____

_____

_____

_____

_____

_____

_____

_____

_____

Hit the Target

But seek first the kingdom of God and his righteousness, and
all these things will be added to you.
— Matthew 6:33

We each have goals we want to reach in life, but it's not enough to have an idea. Once we identify the objective, we must train and equip ourselves to hit the bullseye. In competitive archery, no athlete steps to his mark carrying nothing but a wooden spoon. He takes aim with precisely the gear he needs to control his trajectory. As Christians, we utilize the tools, skills, and relationships God has provided, positioning ourselves in strength and steadiness through Scripture and the Spirit. I can usually tell the difference between someone who has an ambition versus someone who is intentional and persistent in achieving their purpose. How steady is your stance? How strong is your form? Are you strategic about where you go, who you surround yourself with, and what you focus on and do? Position yourself for success by prioritizing the work of the Kingdom of God. Don't just close your eyes, release your arrow, and hope for the best. Steady yourself. Take aim. Be intentional. Transform your dreaming into *doing* by only carrying what keeps you in God's plan. Perfect your form and pursue God first in all you do.

Lord, I pray that You give me the skill, focus, and commitment to hit my target. I offer You my plans that You may have the final say, accomplishing exceedingly above all I can ask or imagine.

_____

_____

_____

_____

_____

_____

_____

_____

_____

_____

_____

_____

_____

_____

_____

_____

_____

_____

_____

_____

ACCELERATE THE PROCESS

For, "Yet a little while, and the coming one will come
and will not delay…
— HEBREWS 10:37

Our times call for us to accelerate in every area. We have been placed on this earth to be salt and light. Like mine, God means for your gifts to advance the Kingdom.

It is said, "time waits for no man," and now more than ever, we need to quit stalling and be about our Father's business. Do you sense the urgency? Pick up the pace on your purpose.

Be intentional about your schedule. Protect your energy, using your God-given talents on God-ordained pursuits. Do not let extra weights slow you down — release the burden of negativity, unforgiveness, and grudges.

Once you genuinely die to your desires, you will advance and accelerate all that is coming to you and through you. Get on board today with what God is doing, and you will see an increase of blessings and be catapulted to a new level.

Lord, Help me be intentional with Your will and not my will. Help me neither hesitate or go ahead of You. I trust Your timing.

_____

_____

_____

_____

_____

_____

_____

_____

_____

_____

_____

_____

_____

_____

_____

_____

_____

_____

_____

FEARLESS

Fear not, for I am with you; be not dismayed, for I am your God; I will strengthen you, I will help you, I will uphold you with my righteous right hand.
— ISAIAH 41:10

Can you imagine how much further along we would be if we were truly fearless followers of Christ? Fear is a cloudy lens giving us an uncertain view of our lives. It has become the go-to response for many who never suffered from anxiety before COVID. Fear and anxiety can derail us, so we must persist in dispelling them from our minds. Author Neale Donald Walsch said, "Fear is False Evidence Appearing Real." Often we allow fear to grow from thoughts and hypothetical catastrophes, paralyzing ourselves from taking the step of faith across the water (Matthew 14:22-23). And we sink. A child may fear being alone, but Isaiah reminds us that we are never abandoned. The enemy wants to isolate us and get us alone. Isn't it encouraging knowing God is with you constantly? And He has placed faithful friends in your life to help watch your blind spot. I can promise you that if you become more aware of God's ever-constant presence, fear will have no room in your heart and mind. You are fearless when you know that you know that you know you are never alone.

Lord, I pray to allow Your perfect love to cast out all my fears (1 John 4:18). Clean my heart and heal me of past hurts so that I may walk in full freedom and faith.

_____

_____

_____

_____

_____

_____

_____

_____

_____

_____

_____

_____

_____

_____

_____

_____

_____

_____

_____

_____

I Can Do All Things

I can do all things through him who strengthens me.
— Philippians 4:13

We know that with Christ, we can do all things — not a few things, not some things —Philippians says, "all things." Many times we forget the completeness of that promise. We try to supplement God's power with vices or people as though there are limits to what God can do. We must move through our days embracing the knowledge that He will not leave one thing out in providing all we need. The Lord is not a man; He does not lie and forget who we are or what we need (Numbers 23:19).

Your Heavenly Father knows your name; He knew you before your parents did. Trust me, your Creator knows what you're capable of. The key phrase in this verse is "through Christ." We can do little in our own strength, our own wisdom, or by our own plan, but through Christ, we can set our expectations high. Expectations set the atmosphere for miracles by increasing how much we can receive. Today, as you face those problematic tasks, remember that God is with you, and His Son purchased your success. Now, watch how He works through you.

Lord, I pray that Christ will always be my chosen source of strength. I will not lean on my understanding, but I will do all You have called me to do.

_____

_____

_____

_____

_____

_____

_____

_____

_____

_____

_____

_____

_____

_____

_____

_____

_____

_____

_____

_____

LIVING

The thief comes only to steal and kill and destroy. I came that they may have life and have it abundantly.
— JOHN 10:10

You may be at a place in your life where you feel you are just going through the motions, living on autopilot. You are not alone. Whether it be career, social life, marriage, or spiritual life, it is not uncommon to find ourselves *just getting by.* Some believers feel like they must restrict themselves from the *fun.* Well, I have news for you — God did not call you to live an ordinary, mundane life. Jesus gave His life so yours would be abundant! He wants you to thrive in your career, be surrounded by extraordinary people, keep the spark going in your marriage, and experience a relationship with Him that is constantly reaching new depths. Do not settle!

If you are not enjoying your life to the fullest, you may need a change, beginning with gratitude. Revisit those areas that may need a makeover and make some alterations if necessary. But remember, you are responsible for choosing joy in each experience. So, stop complaining, stop blaming, stop settling, and start living!

Lord, Help me to do more than survive, but to thrive as Your child. Show me how I may be interfering with the abundant life that You have for me here on earth.

_____

_____

_____

_____

_____

_____

_____

_____

_____

_____

_____

_____

_____

_____

_____

_____

_____

_____

_____

_____

_____

MOMENTUM

But Jesus looked at them and said, "With man this is impossible, but with God all things are possible."
— MATTHEW 19:26

Building and keeping momentum is a big part of creating a steady Battle Rhythm. When we fail to maintain the ground we've obtained, we will not sustain the lifelong change we desire. Change doesn't happen overnight; It is a process. We must be committed to protecting our hard-earned transformation. Momentum is the force or energy gained by continual movement. So, don't stop moving.

Your fuel for the journey is God's Word, prayer, and worship, not only on Wednesday, Sunday, and Christmas but daily. This type of fuel ignites passion within you and creates the drive that keeps you traveling in the right direction. Once you have solid momentum, you will be almost impossible to stop. When an object gains momentum, it creates self-replicating energy, greater force, and speed. In your spiritual life, that means faith makes stronger faith, joy builds grander joy, and peace births more profound peace. It begins with one step, one choice to trust, rejoice, and be confident in your Father's faithfulness. Keep it moving and bust through the chains that try to slow you down.

Lord, I pray for the momentum of progress as I represent Christ in culture.

_____

_____

_____

_____

_____

_____

_____

_____

_____

_____

_____

_____

_____

_____

_____

_____

_____

_____

_____

_____

OPPOSITION IS AN OPPORTUNITY

Not only that, but we rejoice in our sufferings, knowing that suffering produces endurance, and endurance produces character, and character produces hope, and hope does not put us to shame, because God's love has been poured into our hearts through the Holy Spirit who has been given to us.
— ROMANS 5:3-5

When we face opposition, we often run the other way or curl up in a ball. If the fetal position is your battle strategy, you are cheating yourself out of precious opportunities. Opposition creates opportunity. When a butterfly emerges from its chrysalis, the process is challenging, but as it pulls itself through the tiny hole in the cocoon, a hormone is transfused to its wings to strengthen them. If someone were to free the butterfly, it would not have the opportunity to become strong. Without that strength-building struggle, the butterfly would not survive outside the chrysalis. Just like the beautiful butterfly, we need opposition to strengthen and prepare us for whatever is ahead. The apostle Paul knew this. As the verse in Romans tells us, when you are in a struggle, embrace it knowing it produces endurance, character, and hope, which does not disappoint.

Lord, Help me see every situation through Your eyes. I will not isolate myself when confronted by testing trials, but I will draw closer to You and take full advantage of the opportunity within the opposition.

PROGRESS

"But you, take courage! Do not let your hands be weak, for your work shall be rewarded."
— 2 CHRONICLES 15:7

Have you ever felt stuck? Discouraged and disillusioned? One of the biggest causes for a lack of progress is disappointment when reality in no way resembles the picture in our minds. We must learn to align our expectations with God's way and in His time. Author Paulo Coelho said, "When you find your path, you must not be afraid. You need to have sufficient courage to make mistakes. Disappointment, defeat, and despair are the tools God uses to show us the way."[1] Don't be so hard on yourself to make big changes in a short amount of time. Do not allow your expectations to let you down causing you to give up. Now, on the opposite end, if you think you've arrived, you will cease advancing. Why go any further if you've already made it, right? I encourage you to reset your expectations, get unstuck, and keep improving in the things that God has called you to. You don't need all the answers or a map of all the steps. Just put one step of faith in front of the other today and trust God's leading — He knows what He's doing.

Lord, Keep me from making the mistake of thinking that activity means progress. Help me be humble, knowing I will not be completely mature until I see You face to face.

_____

_____

_____

_____

_____

_____

_____

_____

_____

_____

_____

_____

_____

_____

_____

_____

_____

_____

_____

_____

Remember Whose You Are

*And you shall remember the whole way that the Lord your
God has led you these forty years in the wilderness, that he
might humble you, testing you to know what was in your
heart, whether you would keep his commandments or not.*
— Deuteronomy **8:2**

God has created you uniquely, fearfully, and wonderfully
for such a time as this. Wherever you are working,
whoever your family is, whoever your friends are — you
have been called to be a light in the lives of all these people
who have crossed your path. Still, sometimes it can be easy
to lose yourself — forget who you are and *whose* you are.
When crisis after crisis shows up at your front door, you may
ask, *Where is God?* You are not alone. The turmoil of the now
can so consume you; you may forget the many times God has
shown Himself strong in your weakness. No matter what you
are going through, I encourage you to take a moment to stop
and remember the God who brought you through time and
time again and know that if He did it before, He will do it
again. God does not change. He is the same miracle-working
God the Bible describes. Once you have that certainty,
remember that you are His child—chosen, called, and set
apart for His glory. Let that assurance change how you think
and act, inspiring others to know Him, as well.

Lord, Thank You for constantly reminding me that I am Yours and valuable to You. Help me see myself through Your eyes and love myself the way You love me so I can love others more freely and purely.

_____
_____
_____
_____
_____
_____
_____
_____
_____
_____
_____
_____
_____
_____
_____
_____
_____
_____
_____
_____

TRUST THE PROCESS

*Trust in the LORD with all your heart, and do not lean on
your own understanding. In all your ways acknowledge him,
and he will make straight your paths.*
— PROVERBS 3:5-6

Change is a process. To see real, long-lasting change, you must trust the method. Before attempting to alter behavior, surrender to the necessary steps; otherwise, quitting will be just a matter of time. Our culture is used to getting everything fast — fast food, fast internet, fast cars, *everything*. When so much is instant, we don't learn to be persistent. Quality takes time and tenacity. Are you committed to the course? You need to trust God's plan when the journey gets rough and the steps challenging. Count on the process to lead you to the desired destination, despite the headaches along the way. There's no doubt that transformation is inconvenient. The putting off and putting on process is only beneficial if you trust God and His chosen course of action. You are on your way to a better you; God will not lead you astray.

Lord, Give me the strength and courage to trust the process. Help me to grow in patience and gratefulness.

_____
_____
_____
_____
_____
_____
_____
_____
_____
_____
_____
_____
_____
_____
_____
_____
_____
_____
_____
_____
_____

CONSISTENT CONSIDERATION

Set your minds on things that are above, not on things that are on earth.
— COLOSSIANS 3:2

Consideration means to have careful thought, typically over some time. If we were more intentional about how we think, we would make better choices. This does not mean to overthink, but it calls us to think carefully before making certain decisions. Consistent consideration will help us to avoid getting caught up in situations we shouldn't be caught up in. Victorian writer, John Ruskin, said, "Quality is never an accident; it is the result of intentional, intelligent effort."[2] I love that.

We can't assume that we will automatically have quality thinking; we must make consistent effort to monitor our thoughts, build our knowledge, and heighten our wisdom. Minds wander, creating confusion and distractions, but once we utilize constant consideration, we will see the quality of our decisions improve — and with it, the quality of life.

Lord, I surrender my ways to Yours and pray that my mind be renewed and refreshed. I place You in the center of my choices today.

_____

_____

_____

_____

_____

_____

_____

_____

_____

_____

_____

_____

_____

_____

_____

_____

_____

_____

_____

_____

_____

_____

ENJOY THE JOURNEY

For God so loved the world, that he gave his only Son, that whoever believes in him should not perish but have eternal life.
— JOHN 3:16

"Life is like a box of chocolates; you never know what you're gonna get." No one could have said it better than Forrest Gump. Life is tricky with unexpected curveballs — high highs and some really low lows. Whatever may come at me, I'd rather have hard times with Jesus than have good times without Him. Walking with my Father lets me know that no matter what happens, He is with me and has my best interest at heart. He does the same for you. Leave your worries and fears at His feet and enjoy the journey. Life is a gift, but if you spend most of it holding on to past wrongs with their many misinterpreted perspectives, your life will feel like a gift you'd rather return. Have you ever met a person who reeks negativity in every direction? That person is not enjoying the adventure, which is a shame. God gave His Son so that we can live a life of freedom and abundance. Why do we wrap ourselves up again in chains we have already discarded? Your journey is not over even if you feel you were born into a traumatic situation. You can now decide to heal, change your perspective, seek help, turn yourself around, and be a living testimony to others. Enjoy living abundantly the way your Creator intended! No more living in depression and darkness. Change your thinking to start enjoying your journey.

Lord, I will celebrate each step of my journey because I know I am not walking alone — You are guiding my footsteps. I praise You for the peace You bring to my life daily.

_____
_____
_____
_____
_____
_____
_____
_____
_____
_____
_____
_____
_____
_____
_____
_____
_____
_____
_____
_____

GOD IS FIGHTING FOR ME

"…for the LORD your God is he who goes with you to fight for you against your enemies, to give you the victory."
— DEUTERONOMY 20:4

When a boxer steps into the ring, he relies on his training. When it's time for the main event, there are only two in the fight — one man's strength and technique against the other. But when we are in the fight of our lives, we do not face our enemy alone. God and His warring angels surround us. He goes before us to fight our battles, and we need only to be still and know He is God (Psalm 46:10). Are you confident in the outcome of your battle? Do you trust God is working everything to your good — even the punches the enemy manages to land? No matter how many times you slip and fall, God will always be on your side. God is not a man that He would ever walk away when the battle gets heated. No fight is bigger than your Deliverer's power to save. He will stick it out with you through the victory. The result may not always be what you envisioned, but you will come out on top when you allow God to stand up for you. Never put foot in the ring without God by your side. Keep Him with you, and you will "float like a butterfly; sting like a bee"[3] through each round, knowing that God is fighting for you.

Thank you, Lord, for being in my corner, for sorting things out even when I am unaware of how You are moving on my behalf.

_____

_____

_____

_____

_____

_____

_____

_____

_____

_____

_____

_____

_____

_____

_____

_____

_____

_____

_____

_____

_____

Secret Hideout

He who dwells in the shelter of the Most High will abide in the shadow of the Almighty. I will say to the LORD, "My refuge and my fortress, my God, in whom I trust."
— Psalm 91: 1-2

Our Father is a present help and a refuge we can run to at any time; A secret hideout when the storm rages. Gospel singer Karen Clark Sheard sings, "This world sometimes seems cruel and cold and pain doth pierce my very soul, But there's a place, a secret place, A place where I can go. A place of peace, Where love abides, Where justice reigns and God resides, There is a place, A secret place, A place where I can go."[4] A secret is something unknown.

God has a sweet, special place for you to meet with only Him. You know how to get there, and the exchange is intimate in that secret hideout. You can find rest, refreshment, healing, and comfort in this place. You can be vulnerable in a way you cannot be with anyone else. This is a beautiful spot held in your heart with honor. Go there and convene with your Father today, letting Him whisper His sweet secrets in your ear.

Lord, Thank You for being a refuge and fortress. I choose to abide in You, trusting You as my refuge and fortress.

_____
_____
_____
_____
_____
_____
_____
_____
_____
_____
_____
_____
_____
_____
_____
_____
_____
_____
_____
_____
_____
_____
_____

In Line

I delight to do your will, O my God; your law is
within my heart.
— Psalm 40:8

There's a story of a counterfeit agent who, when asked if he had studied a lot of counterfeit money to learn to detect fraudulent bills, shook his head and replied, "No. I study the real thing. If you know what the right thing looks like, you will know how to spot a fake." So many positions and beliefs are screaming for attention, calling us to get in line with them. With those opinions, and our preferences pulling at us, we can risk making catastrophic choices. At times, we can feel so strongly about what we want that we mistake our wants with God's will. We must challenge our beliefs to see how they hold up against the Word of God, continually checking our alignment with God. Even if the way is uncomfortable, we find peace, protection, and progress. Are you longing for that kind of confidence? Moving in line with God's will, you will experience increased faith, knowing that you are protected from the schemes and plans of the enemy. Get ready for doors to open that no man can shut, new opportunities, and progress in your life and for your family, as you choose to be in line with God (Revelation 3:7).

Lord, Help me keep my total being in line with Your will for my life. I desire to know You so well that no trick or trap can fool me.

_____

_____

_____

_____

_____

_____

_____

_____

_____

_____

_____

_____

_____

_____

_____

_____

_____

_____

_____

_____

MARCHING

Now Jericho was shut up inside and outside because of the people of Israel. None went out, and none came in. And the LORD said to Joshua, "See, I have given Jericho into your hand, with its king and mighty men of valor. You shall march around the city, all the men of war going around the city once. Thus shall you do for six days.
— JOSHUA 6:1-3

Author and speaker Jim Rohn, said, "Discipline is the bridge between goals and accomplishment." As we look to better our Battle Rhythms, we must become consistent in patterns and habits that please the Lord. Discipline and consistency are the rhythms you must be marching to. Too many of us are marching to the wrong tempos and wondering why we are tripping over our own two feet, frustrated that we aren't reaching our goals or seeing the change we desire. Anyone who's lived with teenagers knows the stress of hearing different music blaring at you from opposite rooms. It is chaos and confusion and nearly impossible to sing along with one song when another is playing in a different key and tempo with its distinct lyrics and tune. You cannot split your attention between composers to accomplish your objective, sing your song, and march to the rhythm written for you. Concentrate on moving to God's tempo and His alone and stick with it. You will soon find yourself marching to the perfect rhythm through prayer, studying of the Word, receiving the Word, and mentorship. God decreed the Israelites to march around the walled-off city of Jericho to gain victory. March with like-minded believers and see the power of obedience, faith, and unity displayed as the walls around your dreams crumble to the ground.

Lord, Give me the discipline to keep marching no matter the obstacle or the marching orders.

_____

_____

_____

_____

_____

_____

_____

_____

_____

_____

_____

_____

_____

_____

_____

_____

_____

_____

_____

_____

Obey God's Voice

And Samuel said, "Has the LORD as great delight in burnt
offerings and sacrifices, as in obeying the voice of the LORD?
Behold, to obey is better than sacrifice, and to listen
than the fat of rams.
— 1 Samuel 15:22

We hear many voices throughout the day, but being able to distinguish which is God's is the first step toward obedience. The conflicting influences of our family, friends, and mentors, added to the messages from our pasts, can make us doubt our direction. The greatest way to learn to recognize Him is to read His Word; get to know His character and who He is, and you will be able to differentiate His guidance from all the other noise. Then, when you hear, obey.

Following God's instructions shows Him you love Him (John 14:15). It isn't in all the little things you do, your service in the church, or your sacrificial giving. First Samuel tells us that obedience is better than sacrifice. Obey God's voice and watch the blessings fall.

Lord, As I trust in Your Word, give me the ability and the discipline to obey Your still, quiet voice.

_____

_____

_____

_____

_____

_____

_____

_____

_____

_____

_____

_____

_____

_____

_____

_____

_____

_____

_____

RELOADING

*that times of refreshing may come from the presence of the
Lord, and that he may send the Christ appointed for you [...]*
— ACTS 3:20

Each of us needs to take a break from life's day-to-day,
nonstop responsibilities and reload from time to time.
God pours us out, and then He pours right back in. Sometimes
to soak it in, we must step away and sit still with Him. Do
you ever feel like you're on a long stretch of road and your
tank's almost empty? That can be a scary situation. While
traveling the highway, perhaps you've noticed a sign on the
roadside that states *Last Rest Area for 40 Miles.* You look
at your gas gauge, think about that massive cup of coffee
you just guzzled, and know you'd better pull off because
it will be a while before you have a chance again. In life,
taking advantage of rest stops to refresh and restore is how
we maintain our hope and reinforce our patience. Take
some time away to refresh yourself in God. Your family and
friendships will be better for it. Don't busy yourself with all
this stuff and neglect your own needs. Refresh yourself and
delight in the Lord. Once you continue loving people from
a replenished place, you will make such a powerful impact.
Stop living life on *E.* Avoid burnout. Don't ignore your own
needs. Take a look at your fuel gauge, acknowledge the level
you're working from, and take advantage of the signs that
tell you it's time to pull over, refresh, and reload.

Lord, Help me put away my pride and independence to take a break with You. I cannot make this trip without maintaining myself in Your presence where there is fullness of joy.

_____

_____

_____

_____

_____

_____

_____

_____

_____

_____

_____

_____

_____

_____

_____

_____

_____

_____

_____

_____

CURIOSITY

No temptation has overtaken you that is not common to man. God is faithful, and he will not let you be tempted beyond your ability, but with the temptation he will also provide the way of escape, that you may be able to endure it.
— 1 CORINTHIANS 10:13

I'm sure you've heard the proverb, "Curiosity killed the cat," warning of unnecessary investigation or experimentation dangers. Being curious can be a catalyst to learning, but beware — curiosity is often a temptation in disguise. You may not be able to keep the enemy's enticement from trying to lure you to destruction, but it is up to you to take the way out that God provides. If you choose to ignore the escape route thinking you are strong enough to handle it, or you want to see how it will play out, you are playing Russian Roulette. Careless curiosity can cause you to do the very opposite of what the Word instructs. The Bible says to flee the mere appearance of evil, not stick around to see how long it will take before things go sideways (1 Thessalonians 5:22). Curiosity can put you in a dangerous position, flirting with death, be it physical death, the end of a marriage, a friendship, a job, finances, or destroying your health. Don't be like the curious cat. Find that way out and run like your life depends on it.

Lord, May my curiosity lead to creativity aligning with Your will for me and Your Kingdom.

_____

_____

_____

_____

_____

_____

_____

_____

_____

_____

_____

_____

_____

_____

_____

_____

_____

_____

_____

_____

_____

Renewing my Strength

but they who wait for the LORD shall renew their strength;
they shall mount up with wings like eagles; they shall run
and not be weary; they shall walk and not faint.
— Isaiah 40:31

If you want to get back into the race with renewed strength, you must learn how to wait on God. We live in a society of rushers — impatient, lead-footed know-it-alls who want to do things *their* way quicker, faster, and easier. When you wait for God, the outcome is much bigger and better than anything you can make happen. During the wait, God provides you with the proper tools you will need for strength to lift what He has for you. Don't sell yourself short by being too quick to move. Jesus did not give His life just so we can have some knock-off, bootleg imitation of God's best. Something better was intended for you — a blessing that will last. The Lord will unload a blessing you are only able to handle because you accepted the strength-training found in the waiting. Wait on God's timing, and your strength will be renewed.

Lord, Help me remain as my strength is renewed so I can be about Your business.

_____
_____
_____
_____
_____
_____
_____
_____
_____
_____
_____
_____
_____
_____
_____
_____
_____
_____
_____
_____

Know Your Source

The LORD is my strength and my shield; in Him my heart trusts, and I am helped; my heart exults, and with my song I give thanks to Him.
— Psalm 28:7

Today you can walk boldly in authority not because of who you are but because of Christ in you. You can know that He is your strength, your shield, and a sure foundation on which you can build your life. Consistently seek after God, turn away from distraction, and stay in His presence. You can be sure He is a faithful friend who will see you through the most challenging situations. Today, rise and walk in victory, knowing that Jesus Christ is your Lord and Savior. You can speak to mountains and tell them to move without doubt because God is your strength and help in times of trouble. You can know you will not be defeated; you are an overcomer, and your best days are ahead. Don't be tempted to turn to the world, material, or temporary remedies as your source. These things fade away and will leave you empty. Today, be filled with the presence of the Holy Spirit and declare your victory in Jesus' name.

Lord, Thank You for being my source of strength, courage, peace, and protection. I put my trust in You alone.

_____
_____
_____
_____
_____
_____
_____
_____
_____
_____
_____
_____
_____
_____
_____
_____
_____
_____
_____
_____
_____
_____

Consistency

Therefore, my beloved brothers, be steadfast, immovable,
always abounding in the work of the Lord, knowing that in
the Lord your labor is not in vain.
— 1 Corinthians 15:58

Little shifts add up to significant change. When we are consistent with continual, meaningful time with the Lord, we will propel our faith, restore our hope, and cause joy to overflow. While expecting others to be dependable, many of us can admit to repeatedly failing in our commitment to being consistent with the Lord. We are human, but I never want to be the reason someone believes Christians are hypocrites. John chapter 8 tells the story of the woman caught in adultery: While Jesus was worshipping in the temple, the religious leaders, wanting to see Christ's reaction, reminded Him that the law says adultery is punishable by stoning. Jesus graciously replied, "He that is without sin among you, let him throw the first stone." One by one, each accuser left the scene. With the same type of judgment we express at times, these men wanted her to pay the price for her sin, but they were unwilling to deal with their own (John 8:1-44). Today, I challenge you to set the standard for faithfulness, check yourself first, and show grace to others. Spending consistent time with God will give you the strength to love consistently and forgive consistently. When your words match your actions, every area of your life begins to improve. Glorify God by becoming dependable, reliable, and faithful.

Lord, Help me be consistent in every area of my life. Make me a productive and fruitful ambassador of Christ, forgiving others when they fall short.

_____

_____

_____

_____

_____

_____

_____

_____

_____

_____

_____

_____

_____

_____

_____

_____

_____

_____

_____

_____

_____

God's Positioning

But seek first the kingdom of God and his righteousness, and
all these things will be added to you.
— Matthew 6:33

Our God is an on-time God. It's not by accident that doors are opening in your life, windows are being pushed up, and connections are being made. If you seek after God, He will line up resources, contacts, and finances for you and your family. But when you focus on *your* plans first, it can cause confusion and delay. God's blessings are generational, and His desire is for you to succeed in your endeavors while bringing glory to Him. Gideon thought he had it all together. Facing a war with 20,000 men, he believed he had all he needed to win the battle; but God wanted him to be victorious *with the realization that God was the reason for it.*

Today, put your focus on the Lord and allow Him to work it all out. Do not be fearful or self-sufficient. The Lord, your God, is with you and positioning you for a win that honors Him.

Lord, Today I will consciously decide to keep You at the center of my life.

_____
_____
_____
_____
_____
_____
_____
_____
_____
_____
_____
_____
_____
_____
_____
_____
_____
_____
_____
_____
_____

STRENGTH IN STRUCTURE

But all things should be done decently and in order.
— 1 CORINTHIANS 14:40

The strength of a military force is displayed in its ability to fight a war, gaining and protecting ground. But without following proper formation, their plans will fail. Likewise, the strength of our faith is proven in discipline to structure our plan according to God's will. In my experience, God gives a vision for where we're going, and He instructs us on the next step, but little else at the start. The entire journey between start and finish is a mystery, only being revealed one step of obedience at a time.

When the Lord told Abraham of His plans for him, Abraham couldn't see how he would possess the land God promised him. Still, he obeyed. Have you ever struggled with doubt? If you are going through a tough time, remember God's promise for you is the same as it was for Abraham — "I am your shield, your exceedingly great reward" (Genesis 15:1). Prove your faith by taking the next step.

Lord, Help me be transparent with my doubts and fears, knowing You will respond with encouragement, love, and clear direction.

_____

_____

_____

_____

_____

_____

_____

_____

_____

_____

_____

_____

_____

_____

_____

_____

_____

_____

_____

_____

God Is in Control

*The heart of man plans his way, but the LORD
establishes his steps.*
— Proverbs 16:9

It is a beautiful thing to be completely sure that God has a plan for each of us, and His plans never fail. Maybe you're facing unsettling memories of your past, insecurities in your job, or questions about your family's direction. Perhaps a doctor suddenly gave you some disappointing news. Whatever unwanted or unexpected event shakes you, you can count on God and His promises. Seek Him and let Him be your light in the darkness and your joy in times of sorrow. God is your great counselor when you feel lost or unmotivated. Your gracious, loving Father knows what you need, how to supply it, and when to bestow it. The Almighty establishes your steps and works everything out to your benefit (Romans 8:28). There is no losing with your Creator in control of things.

Lord, Give me the fortitude to go on in courage, knowing You are in control.

Victory

But thanks be to God, who gives us the victory through our Lord Jesus Christ.
— 1 Corinthians 15:57

Lift your head and stand your ground; "Be steadfast, immovable, always abounding in the work of the Lord, knowing you do not labor in vain" (1 Corinthians 15:58). Do not give in to the temptation of doubt and discouragement. In Daniel 3, Shadrach, Meshach, and Abednego faced a death sentence when they chose to pray to our God, disobeying the orders of King Nebuchadnezzar. The three men put their faith in God, refusing to deny Him, knowing it would result in their deaths by fiery furnace. After being in the 1800-degree furnace for a time, a guard peered in. Expecting to see nothing but ashes, he saw not three but four men, much alive, standing untouched by the flame. God saved them and stood in their midst. When you stand up for God, He will stand up for you, and people will come to know Him because of your faith and courage.

Lord, Thank You for my victory through the life, death, and resurrection of Jesus Christ. I will arm myself in worship, knowing You win every battle.

Pathway

You make known to me the path of life; in your presence there is fullness of joy; at your right hand are pleasures forevermore.
—Psalm 16:11

Do the voices in your head say you will never make it? If you ever feel confused about where you're going and all looks lost, remember that your steps are put in order by the Lord (Psalm 37:23). When panic sets in and choices are complicated, turn to your Heavenly Father. He cares so much about you; He will go to the ends of the earth to find you, redirect you, and bring you back into His loving arms. In the parable of the lost sheep, Jesus told a story of a shepherd with one-hundred sheep who lost one. The shepherd stopped what he was doing and began to search for the one missing lamb until he found it. Lifting it up, and putting it upon his shoulders, he began to rejoice as he returned it to the other ninety-nine (Luke 15). Likewise, our Father will pick you up, boost you to His capable shoulders, and bring you back to the fold. When you are disoriented and weary and have wandered off, call to the Good Shepherd. He waits with open arms.

Lord, I am not asking for an easy path but for You to light my way. Never let me stray from Your pasture.

_____

_____

_____

_____

_____

_____

_____

_____

_____

_____

_____

_____

_____

_____

_____

_____

_____

_____

_____

Don't Blame the Shovel

So then each of us will give an account of himself to God.
— Romans 14:12

If, after years of unhealthy choices and dangerous digging, you are shocked every time a trench appears; if you blame your background or circumstances or others whenever you're lying at the bottom of the consequences you carved out for yourself, do not expect much to change. But if you want to start seeing progress and experience the peace of maturity, acknowledge where you went wrong and what you can do to add and eliminate whatever brings you closer to the character of Christ. Author Craig D. Lounsbrough said, "When I'm at the bottom looking up, the main question may not be 'how do I get out of this hole?' In reality, the main question might be 'how do I get rid of the shovel that I used to dig it?"[5] I challenge you today to illuminate and eliminate whatever you have used to dig ditches of disappointment for yourself. Identify the thoughts, words, beliefs, and choices that chipped away at your solid ground until it fell away beneath you. You are responsible for picking up the shovel of habits, relationships, and negative thinking that creates your pit of destruction, depression, or depletion. Your success and happiness may be more within your control than you realize. It's up to you.

Lord, I pray that you place individuals in my life that will hold me accountable to Your will for me and not my own.

_____
_____
_____
_____
_____
_____
_____
_____
_____
_____
_____
_____
_____
_____
_____
_____
_____
_____
_____
_____
_____

LISTENING TO HIS DIRECTION

When the Spirit of truth comes, he will guide you into all the truth, for he will not speak on his own authority, but whatever he hears he will speak, and he will declare to you the things that are to come.
— JOHN 16:13

Praise God that we do not have to live in this world drifting and purposeless. Under God's authority, the Holy Spirit guides us every step. Whether four or ninety-four, all of us have plenty to learn, even when we think we know it all. I have good news for you — God has more in store. Keep your spiritual ears open. Are you the researcher, the curious person constantly looking to learn more? Or are you bored and stagnant in your walk? I encourage you to allow the Lord to speak into your life. Seek Him out, and don't let go until you get the answers you need. Notice I said *need,* not *want.* Each of us has the potential to grow in our love for the Lord and our knowledge of Him. I encourage you to engage with Almighty God in worship; speak to Him through prayer, and listen to His voice. Although others may have steered you the wrong way, you can count on God to never fail you. Listen to Him. Let His Spirit guide your steps and guard your heart.

Lord, I give thoughtful attention to Your direction; give me the courage to respond accordingly.

LISTEN TO THE BEAT

*My sheep hear my voice, and I know them, and they follow
me. I give them eternal life, and they will never perish, and no
one will snatch them out of my hand.*
— JOHN 10:27-28

Absorbing the Word of God and spending time in His
presence is the most life-altering, faith-strengthening
habit for the believer. Do it, and you will find out that
the more you listen intently, the clearer you will hear the
heartbeat of God. When you spend time in the presence of
the Lord without distractions, giving Him your full attention,
the Spirit will remind you that you are the Lord's beloved
child. King David expresses his love for God throughout
the Psalms. He was certain God heard him because God had
"inclined his ear" to him (Psalm 116:2). David promised to
call upon God all the days of his life.

Today, I ask you to commit to two things: *Show up* and
Surrender. Slow down and hear the heartbeat of God today.
When you walk to the beat of God's rhythm, you can be
assured that He will empower you to live and love like Jesus.

Lord, Help me to prioritize time with You to build our relationship. I commit to giving more attention to thankfulness and promise to be still and listen.

_____

_____

_____

_____

_____

_____

_____

_____

_____

_____

_____

_____

_____

_____

_____

_____

_____

_____

_____

_____

_____

_____

FLEXIBLE

Do not be conformed to this world, but be transformed by the renewal of your mind, that by testing you may discern what is the will of God, what is good and acceptable and perfect.
—ROMANS 12:2

Many of us begin our day with an idea of how we will spend it, only to get dragged in an unexpected direction. We tend to identify the intruder as a distraction, but what if the interruption is actually God's *redirection*. Michael McGriff is credited as saying, "Blessed are the flexible, for they will not be bent out of shape." Sometimes, God will allow hardships to enter our well-planned schedule to shift our course and change our attention and direction. Remind yourself that distractions are often God's redirection. We must be willing to change course for His desired path. When God says *no*, it may not be forever; the delay might only be for now. Always remember that the plans God has for you are better than the ones you create. Let God take the lead and embrace His desires for your day. Ask the Lord to help you become flexible with your ideas and allow God to take complete control.

Lord, Give me the discipline to adapt and adjust as You lead me. Help me to loosen my grip on my itinerary.

_____

_____

_____

_____

_____

_____

_____

_____

_____

_____

_____

_____

_____

_____

_____

_____

_____

_____

_____

_____

FOLLOW THE CAPTAIN

"Shout! For the Lord has given you the city!"
— JOSHUA 6:16B

Most of us realize we will face barriers on the journey to the blessing. We prepare ourselves for naysayers and financial hurdles and pick ourselves up after moments of doubt and discouragement. We expect struggles between the start and the success of our dreams and goals, but we are working toward something great, so we press on. Many of us are not prepared, however when the promise is fulfilled and full of its own set of problems and pains. The children of Israel traveled four decades to the land that was promised to them and quickly realized what I'm sure you know by now — after you work to achieve your *dream come true,* you must wrestle to keep it. The book of Joshua describes the seven years of settlement of the land of Israel after seven years of battles, starting with the Jericho conquest (Joshua 6:1-20). The captain of that battle was the Lord of Hosts, Himself (Joshua 15), with specific instructions. When God's people followed their marching orders (literally), the walls around the fortified city crumbled, giving them access to the blessings within. You see, God is not supporting *our* plans; we are supporting *His.* It is the cause of Christ for which we sacrifice and surrender, not our own preferred purposes and projects. Give up control of the timing and tempo of your march, and you will see the barriers fall as the Lord's promise unfolds.

Lord, Prepare me for the task at hand and the responsibility of taking hold of Your promise. I will obey Your instructions and release the specifics to Your command.

_____
_____
_____
_____
_____
_____
_____
_____
_____
_____
_____
_____
_____
_____
_____
_____
_____
_____
_____
_____

GOD-GUIDANCE

For that is what God is like. He is our God forever and ever,
And he will guide us until we die.
— PSALMS 48:14, NLT

S ome choices are simple — what's for dinner, which shoes to wear. Then there are the routes that come down to more than preferences. When facing decisions like a job change, a new business venture, or relationships, we need wisdom and guidance from someone who sees farther than any other advisor. David cried out to the Lord for guidance many times. "Show me the right path, oh Lord; Point out the road for me to follow" (Psalm 25:4). People are usually well-meaning, but even when giving good advice, they will not join us on the journey to see it through. When we seek our Heavenly Father's direction, not only does He give us the counsel, but He walks with us through it all. Through the Word of God, we position ourselves to open up our spiritual ears in our prayer, fasting, and worship. Are you tired of arguing, tossing, and turning? Next time you feel a little out of sorts about a life decision, pause and pray. You have the Holy Spirit to guide you. You never need to take on the world alone. Release the pressure, pause, and listen. Allow the Good Shepherd to lead you.

Lord, Help me submit as You guide me on this life's tour.

_____

_____

_____

_____

_____

_____

_____

_____

_____

_____

_____

_____

_____

_____

_____

_____

_____

_____

_____

ADVANCE

Not that I have already obtained this or am already perfect, but I press on to make it my own, because Christ Jesus has made me his own. Brothers, I do not consider that I have made it my own. But one thing I do: forgetting what lies behind and straining forward to what lies ahead, I press on toward the goal for the prize of the upward call of God in Christ Jesus.
—PHILIPPIANS 3:12-14

Today, invite the Lord into a specific area of your life to help you grow. Who better to learn from? Spiritual growth depends on the willingness to only advance on God's revelations through the Holy Spirit's leading. You may not always agree with God's timing or technique; however, you can pray to the Lord to increase your trust in Him as you grow through your circumstances. Because faith comes by hearing the Word of God, ask the Lord to open your heart and spiritual ears so that you are confident going forward (Romans 10:17). When a military force advances toward their enemy, they are securing ground. Move forward through consistent, scheduled time in the Word; worship the Lord, and stay connected through the local church, serving the body. Glorify God and do not settle for last year's ordinary. It's time to advance in your faith, commitment, and calling in the Lord.

Lord, As I advance in taking territory for Your Kingdom, teach me how to build and defend.

_____

_____

_____

_____

_____

_____

_____

_____

_____

_____

_____

_____

_____

_____

_____

_____

_____

_____

_____

_____

Change Up

Follow all the directions the Lord has given you. Then life will go well for you.
—Deuteronomy 5:33

Life is not linear. Our path has twists and turns, obstacles and detours that will require us to pivot. What got you here won't necessarily take you there. God is constantly moving; we need to move with Him, shifting course, changing tracks, and be willing to do new things to accomplish His will. Change can be difficult; we are creatures who enjoy our comfort. You'd better be ready when God has a path you didn't plan on — like Jonah. When Jonah rebelled and sailed off in the opposite direction of God's command, he put his life in danger and everyone else's. Ultimately, he was thrown overboard, but God, in His grace and mercy, sent a big fish to swallow Jonah and bring him to safety. God gave Jonah another chance, and this time, *this* time he obeyed. Jonah's willingness to repent and follow God's way led him to the people of Nineveh, whose evilness had broken the heart of God. Because of the warning, the people repented and cried out for God's help. Jonah's willingness to change impacted a nation for God (Jonah 3). Today, ask God to help you trust Him when His way is uncomfortable. Trust the process.

Lord, Help me not to allow stubbornness to rob me of the changes required to become the best version of myself.

_____

_____

_____

_____

_____

_____

_____

_____

_____

_____

_____

_____

_____

_____

_____

_____

_____

_____

_____

THE TWO EDGED SWORD

For the word of God is living and active, sharper than any two-edged sword, piercing to the division of soul and of spirit, of joints and of marrow, and discerning the thoughts and intentions of the heart.
— HEBREWS 4:12

The Word of God will enter where no other sword can. It is alive and active, making critical dissections to cut away our soulish, fleshly nature. It pierces the soul (the flesh) and its unhealthy habits while cutting, curing, and correcting our character. The Word of God dissects pride and perversion and leaves a spirit of humility and obedience. Are you struggling to remove destructive habits and thoughts from your life? I encourage you to consume the Scripture like you would a prescribed medication which has proven to ease your suffering. Those habits that have become like second nature, deeply rooted, will be dug up and cut off by this sword. Do you desire wisdom? God's Holy Word will cut away ignorance and confusion, leaving you with understanding and clear direction. If your thoughts have turned against you, the Sword of the Spirit will divide "joints and marrow," the most intimate parts of your being, discerning the intent of your heart and your most secret thoughts and desires. Let the Word of God reveal, remove, and repair all that you are to become all that your Creator designed you to be.

Lord, Show me my "disease." I am willing to undergo Your intimate and invasive spiritual surgery to be whole and clean in Your sight.

_____

_____

_____

_____

_____

_____

_____

_____

_____

_____

_____

_____

_____

_____

_____

_____

_____

_____

_____

_____

_____

_____

BREAST PLATE OF RIGHTEOUSNESS

and whatever we ask we receive from him, because we keep
his commandments and do what pleases him.
— 1 JOHN 3:22

In the same way a bulletproof vest or body armor protects a soldier or police officer's heart and vital organs against whatever weapons come against him, righteousness guards us against our enemy's attacks. We are made in right-standing with God through the blood of Christ at the moment of salvation; we remain safeguarded through our obedience to the Lord. Righteousness is "acting according to a proper (God's) standard, doing what is right, being in the right." If you desire to pursue God and seek to live in accordance with His will, you will find fulfillment. Matthew 5:6 says, "Blessed are those who hunger and thirst for righteousness, for they shall be satisfied." Righteousness comes only from God, but it is not a one-off. Once you are saved, the Holy Spirit will direct you away from sin and toward right living. When you face temptation, you can guard your heart against the devil's schemes and avoid capture by operating according to the Lord's commands. Righteousness is your bulletproof vest for whatever comes at you today. Put it on.

Lord, I pray for the strength to obey Your commands and live in a way that is honorable to You.

_____

_____

_____

_____

_____

_____

_____

_____

_____

_____

_____

_____

_____

_____

_____

_____

_____

_____

_____

Fighting Words

Therefore I tell you, whatever you ask in prayer, believe that you have received it, and it will be yours.
— Mark 11:24

When life takes a jab at you, how do you counter? What is your response when stress and circumstances whiz by you rapid-fire? Do you curl up in a ball of anxiety and depression? Does your mouth shoot off words of frustration? Or do you commit to firing declarations of faith at your situation? You have collected the Word in your heart. Now, march through the enemy's camp with praise as your battle cry, and prepare to possess the land. Stand up! Advance! You are on the winning side even if you feel outgunned and outnumbered by financial instability, relationship troubles, personal insecurities, or simply too much work and not enough hours or energy. So, act like it. Declare the goodness of the Lord; announce what He has done and who He is in you and through you. Shout out your fighting words of faith and see the victory the Lord will bring you today!

Lord, I will keep Your Word in my heart, stockpiled and ready for battle.

_____

_____

_____

_____

_____

_____

_____

_____

_____

_____

_____

_____

_____

_____

_____

_____

_____

_____

_____

_____

_____

In Step

*and though a man might prevail against one who is alone,
two will withstand him — a threefold cord
is not quickly broken.*
— Ecclesiastes 4:12

From China to the United States, militaries display their formation in parades. A 2014 study by the University of California showed marching in unison causes people to judge "their potential opponents as less formidable than men who didn't walk in unison." In fact, the man cast as an "enemy" was viewed as shorter and smaller by the men who marched together than by those who marched independently. The men who walked alone saw this enemy as dangerous, while the group believed him to be of no real threat. There is a saying, "There is strength in numbers," meaning a group of people has more influence and power than one person alone. We were made to need each other, to "aim for restoration, comfort one another, agree with one another, live in peace" (2 Corinthians 13:11). The Bible tells us to "not give up meeting together" (Hebrews 10:25), "for the body does not consist of one member but of many" (1 Corinthians 12:14). If you're facing more than a little skirmish, march into battle with other well-trained, like-minded Christians. Make a commitment to yourself and your family today to get connected to a local body of believers.

Lord, I put away all my excuses. Lead me to church and give me the heart to serve and connect in a real way with my brothers and sisters.

Thought Process of a Soldier

No soldier gets entangled in civilian pursuits, since his aim is to please the one who enlisted him.
— 2 Timothy 2:4

A good soldier does not go rogue. Before the day attacks you with all of its demands, consult God. Your Heavenly Father is waiting to hear your praises and your needs. Every step of life's journey holds decisions that will determine your future. It's up to you to make sure you don't take off without the commission of your Commander.

Meet with Him daily, early in the morning when you first awaken but make sure you are not doing all the talking.

Listen to receive your orders, so you don't trip up when you fall out into the day.

Seek God for your family, business, dreams, and plans.

Above all, keep your mind on Heavenly pursuits and Godly interests, not allowing yourself to get distracted by things of this world.

Lord, Help me not head into my day without marching orders. I will stop and listen before acting.

_____

_____

_____

_____

_____

_____

_____

_____

_____

_____

_____

_____

_____

_____

_____

_____

_____

_____

_____

_____

_____

A Soldiers Strength

Be strong and courageous. Do not fear or be in dread of them, for it is the LORD your God who goes with you. He will not leave you or forsake you.
— Deuteronomy 31:6

A soldier has a strength that has been refined over time through training and intensive experiences. God gives us the same opportunity to have a power rooted deep within us that we can constantly draw from. We build our strength through adversity, crisis, study, prayer, fasting, fellowship, and service.

Life is experienced in levels and arrives in stages; we cannot progress through the ranks of purpose without increasing our strength. Stand firm; Be wise. Trust God through each challenge in transformation.

God intends for you to have a soldier's strength, rooted in Him, never failing, even in the face of adversity.

Lord, I commit to the training and discipline required to develop a soldier's strength, equipped to carry Your banner.

_____

_____

_____

_____

_____

_____

_____

_____

_____

_____

_____

_____

_____

_____

_____

_____

_____

_____

_____

_____

Staying Steady

*Therefore, my beloved brothers, be steadfast, immovable,
always abounding in the work of the Lord, knowing that in
the Lord your labor is not in vain.*
— 1 Corinthians 15:58

By definition, *steadfast* means to "be resolutely or dutifully firm and unwavering." This is a key quality to possess as Christians in today's world. Everywhere we turn distractions are trying to pull us left and right and off track. To remain in step with God, we must work to become firm and faithful. You and I must commit to it and stick to it.

When you set out to do something, see it all the way and do not waver, even when the thrill is gone. Do not be deceived by ulterior solutions that seem quick and easy. You are not of the world, so follow God's Word and stay steadfast in Him and all you do.

Lord, I pray for perseverance and unwavering faith to stay steadfast to Your plans for my life.

_____

_____

_____

_____

_____

_____

_____

_____

_____

_____

_____

_____

_____

_____

_____

_____

_____

_____

_____

_____

The Faithfulness of the Father

*Know therefore that the LORD your God is God, the faithful
God who keeps covenant and steadfast love with those who
love him and keep his commandments,
to a thousand generations...*
— Deuteronomy 7:9

God has many names and plays many roles in our lives, but I believe the sweetest is that of a father. If you did not have the best experience with your earthly dad, you might find it difficult to see God as faithful and loving. But your Heavenly Father is unlike any temporal relationship you have ever had. He is faithful. He is committed. He is in it for the long haul.

So many people will come and go in your life, but God, your Father, will never leave or forsake you (Hebrews 13:5). His love will follow you to the gates of hell, snatch you from death, and set your spirit on the highest mountaintop. There is nowhere you can go that God is not there, and there is nothing you can do to make Him give up on you. You can count on Him. Your Father walks with you hand-in-hand, so you never have to feel alone. Remember, God the Father is faithful, and His love will never fail.

Lord. Today I dedicate my whole life, everything I am, to You as my father.

_____
_____
_____
_____
_____
_____
_____
_____
_____
_____
_____
_____
_____
_____
_____
_____
_____
_____
_____
_____

COMMIT TO THE PROCESS

Commit your way to the LORD; trust in him, and he will act.
— PSALM 37:5

We set a goal. We make a plan. We start strong. And then... Too often, between starting and succeeding, we give up. When the task becomes inconvenient, challenging, or lengthy, we can become overwhelmed without the proper support or resources. Change doesn't happen overnight. We must keep to the course — commit to the process by preparing.

Winston Churchill said, "He who fails to plan, plans to fail." Develop a strategy and include people and sources who will get behind you, loan their experience, and hold you accountable along the way. Draw from God's strength and wisdom and keep moving to His battle rhythm. Giving up will be unlikely as you keep to the course and commit to the process.

Lord, I am fully engaged and ask for strength and discipline in the follow-through as I commit to what You set before me.

SPIRITUAL AWARENESS

He said, "Do not be afraid, for those who are with us are more than those who are with them."
— 2 KINGS 6:16

The Bible clarifies that there is an active spiritual realm where God and His warring angels are moving on our behalf. The Apostle Paul wrote, "For in him [the Son of God] all things were created: things in heaven and on earth, visible and invisible, whether thrones or powers or rulers or authorities; all things have been created through him and for him" (Colossians 1:16, NIV). Today, make it a point to look beyond the obvious to the purpose in each interaction, every situation. Cultivate your spiritual awareness through your relationship with the Holy Spirit, God's Spirit, who communicates with your spirit. No matter the noise, chaos, and confusion that may be spinning around you, you can develop the internal stillness that allows you to hear the small voice of insight and direction. Jesus told His disciples that "When the Spirit of truth comes, he will guide you into all truth, for he will not speak on his own authority, but whatever he hears he will speak, and he will declare to you the things that are to come" (John 16:13). Ask the Lord to do for you what He performed for Elisha's servant. The servant woke to find them under attack by Syria's army. He was in a panic, but the prophet was calm and confident. Elisha asked God to open his servant's eyes so the terrified man could see what Elisha's spiritual awareness revealed – "the mountain was full of horses and chariots of fire" protecting Elisha. Today, actively pursue a consciousness only given by God through His Spirit.

Lord, Open my eyes and ears so I can see beyond my physical sight, and hear Your quiet voice leading me.

Understanding and Knowledge

For the LORD gives wisdom; from his mouth come
knowledge and understanding;
— Proverbs 2:6

Knowledge does not equal understanding. Does that statement surprise you? Many believe the terms mean essentially the same thing, but they do not. The Bible tells us so. In the verse above, there are three separate Hebrew words for *wisdom, knowledge*, and *understanding*, all with distinct definitions. Knowledge (da'at) and understanding (tbûnâ), meaning information and insight, come from the Word of the Lord. He gives us the facts and the ability to draw meaning from the facts; the resulting wisdom (ḥokmâ) directs us in what to do next — the skill and ability to apply the knowledge and understanding in the right way, at the perfect time. None of these vital characteristics just happen. We must seek after them with all our hearts. Theologian RC Sproul said, "Our Lord calls for a continued application of the mind to His Word. A disciple does not dabble in learning. He makes the pursuit of an understanding of God's Word a chief business of his life."[6] To walk in wisdom, you must be a disciple, a follower. Passionately chase after the heart of God today.

Lord, As I pursue Your heart, give me knowledge and understanding of Your Word that I will walk in Your wisdom.

_____

_____

_____

_____

_____

_____

_____

_____

_____

_____

_____

_____

_____

_____

_____

_____

_____

_____

_____

_____

_____

_____

Prove It

But someone will say, "You have faith and I have works."
Show me your faith apart from your works, and I will show
you my faith by my works.
— James 2:18

For followers of Christ, salvation's response is obedience. Our faith makes way for proven results. James makes it clear that while nothing can save us but the blood of Christ, our salvation and faith in God will result in a tangible outcome. When Peter had faith, he walked on water — until he didn't. When Joshua believed God, he obeyed his directive, and the walls of Jericho bowed to him. When Abraham had faith, he was willing to do the unfathomable until God let him off the hook and spared Isaac. When Hannah had faith, she kept after the Lord until He gave her a child. What results have you seen from your faith?

Faith is knowing God can do it. Trust is relying on Him as you jump, knowing He will either catch you or teach you to fly. The deeds that come from our faith require a trust in God that is proven in action. You say you have faith? Prove it.

Lord, Help me to be obedient to Your Word, and rely on You, proving my faith through my choices and actions.

_____

_____

_____

_____

_____

_____

_____

_____

_____

_____

_____

_____

_____

_____

_____

_____

_____

_____

_____

_____

IDENTIFY

So, whether you eat or drink, or whatever you do, do all to the glory of God.
— 1 CORINTHIANS 10:31

In the New Testament, believers did not refer to themselves as *Christians*. Some scholars believe the term was derogatory at a time when the Greeks gave satirical nicknames to particular groups, usually political. Proponents of Nero Augustus were called "Augustinians;" General Sulla's followers were "Sullanians." Then a bunch popped up in Antioch whose behaviors and speech centered on Christ, and the Greeks called them "Christians." As it was then, so it is now. People will know you are Christ's only if you show that you are Christ's. In our culture, we give and are given labels for all sorts of reasons — skills and spills, reality and rumor, virtues, as well as vices. We are pigeon-holed by our skin, our kin, and the crowd we're in. If your primary identity is about anything other than who God says you are as His child, you are selling yourself short. Do not rob yourself or others of seeing what's most important when they look at you — the image of a loving, omnipotent, powerful God.

Lord, As I put on the mind of Christ, transform me into Your image. Help me to put my identity as Your child above any other label.

Divine Wisdom

*But the wisdom from above is first pure, then peaceable,
gentle, open to reason, full of mercy and good fruits,
impartial and sincere.*
— James 3:17

Albert Einstein said, "Knowledge is realizing that the street is one way; wisdom is looking in both directions anyway."[7] Human wisdom comes from education and experience — insights and responses we have picked up along the way in life's journey. We get it by learning from our mistakes or accepting the hard-learned lessons of our grandparents. It is valuable, and yet, there is superior wisdom that is beyond human knowledge or understanding — more insightful and intuitive than a lifetime of experiences could teach. Divine wisdom is sourced from God, Himself, with the characteristics listed plainly in the third chapter of the book of James: *pure, peaceable, gentle, reasonable, merciful, produces good fruits, sincere and impartial.* I know from experience that God's wisdom often comes in the form of surrender, humility, and silence at a moment when you may want to scream, argue, and plead your case. Look at the many Old Testament battles when wars were won in ways which seemed contrary to a successful strategy. Kings can establish a battle plan; seasoned military men can train and carry out a strategy according to human wisdom. But when God steps in and says, "Be still," or "March around these walls," victory is in the obedience to directions that may even seem illogical. Today, ask the Lord to give you a wisdom beyond human understanding, and obey His direction. Do it, and you will see a victory.

Lord, You said You would give wisdom to all who ask. I am asking now for the gift of Your wisdom in my situation today.

GOD'S PEACE AND JOY

May the God of hope fill you with all joy and peace in believing, so that by the power of the Holy Spirit you may abound in hope.
— ROMANS 15:13

Stop right now and celebrate the victories God has won in your life. Look back and see the faithfulness of the Lord. What valley did God lift you from? What storm did He settle in your life? What mountaintop experience has He provided to your family? Focus today on the promises of God and settle your heart with the peace and joy He gives. When you need strength for your current trial, I encourage you to celebrate God's goodness. Call out to the Lord and praise Him. He is the God that renews, restores, and rebuilds. If you feel challenged by your current situation remember the words of King David in Psalm 28:7, "The Lord is my strength and my shield; in him my heart trusts, and I am helped; my heart exults, and with my song I give thanks to him." Although David faced many troubles and often felt like giving up when his enemies surrounded him, David put his trust in the Lord. David praised God in the good times and bad. Only God can fill your heart with joy and surround you with a peace beyond your understanding. You can count on that same peace right now. Begin to celebrate the goodness of the Lord and verbalize your praise to the highest God.

Lord, Your praise will continually be in my mouth as I celebrate Your goodness at all times, in all things.

THE CHANGE IS FOREVER

Therefore, my beloved brothers, be steadfast, immovable, always abounding in the work of the Lord, knowing that in the Lord your labor is not in vain. — 1 CORINTHIANS 15:58

The Marines have a saying: "The change is forever," meaning *once a Marine, always a Marine.* The principles, training, ideals, willingness, and determination cannot waver or wain from one day to the next. So it is with our commitment to live God's call on our lives. Consistency is key.

The dictionary defines consistency as the "steadfast adherence to the same principles, course, form, etc."[8] When we are consistent, people can depend on us. Do your friends and family know they can trust you to maintain your integrity and character? Or are they never sure from one instance to the next which *you* will show up to a situation?

Stick to your word, remain steady, and achieve a meaningful life of value and peace. Stand on the truth of God's Word and faith in His character, and your character will hold no matter the difficulties, dilemmas, or flat-out disasters you will undoubtedly face through the years. Are you a child of God, chosen for such a time as this for His purposes and pleasure? Stand firm. Keep your mind set on things above, respond in love, personify grace, choose according to the values of Christ, and walk in integrity. The Change is Forever.

Lord, I will follow Your Spirit's lead in all situations, consistently responding and reaching in love, grace, and integrity.

_____

_____

_____

_____

_____

_____

_____

_____

_____

_____

_____

_____

_____

_____

_____

_____

_____

_____

_____

_____

_____

_____

Loyal to the End

A friend loves at all times, and a brother is born for adversity.
— Proverbs 17:17

There is little that proves our loyalty better than how we respect and protect each other's reputations. When a potentially embarrassing moment arises for someone in leadership over you, do you protect the reputation or will you propagate the rumor?

After the flood waters had receded, Noah planted a vineyard and drank some wine one evening. Ham, his youngest son, found him passed out and naked inside his tent. Rather than protecting his dad's reputation, he told his brothers. Understand that in Noah's time, the father held a position of great honor in the family. To witness Noah in a vulnerable position and then to talk about it was to bring shame on him deliberately. When Ham told the older two, out of respect, Shem and Japheth, out of respect, they wouldn't even look at their father in that condition. Instead, they put a blanket over their shoulders and backed into the room to cover their father's indiscretion. They protected Noah's reputation and defended his position in their own eyes. Martin Luther said, "Where the battle rages, there the loyalty of the soldier is proved." In your relationships with family, friends, and especially leaders, their position must be protected and honored even when the person is imperfect. It all comes down to who you are. Are you a person of honor?

Heavenly Father, make me a person of honor who protects the reputations of my leaders. I will not disrespect Your chosen ones.

Stockpiled Faith

And rising very early in the morning, while it was still dark,
he departed and went out to a desolate place, and there he
prayed. — Mark *1:35*

When COVID went global in March 2020, Google searches on prayer skyrocketed.[9] The world recognized the 75th anniversary of the end of World War II that same year. As we reflected, we noticed the same type of response as three-fourths of Americans, affected by the horrors of war, joined a house of worship in 1945.[10] We are in a battle; we have been since Adam and Eve's disobedience, and as any soldier or Boy Scout knows, we must "Be Prepared."

The Gospel of Mark gives the account of a desperate father who brings his son to be delivered from an unclean spirit that caused the boy to be unable to hear or speak. After driving out the spirits and healing the boy, the disciples asked the Rabbi why they had failed to heal him when they attempted it. Jesus replied, "This kind cannot be driven out by anything but prayer and fasting" (Mark 9). When Jesus encountered the boy, He didn't need to stop and pray or take a day or two without food before He could heal him. Why? In a battle, the soldiers do not run to the armory to get their guns and ammunition when the enemy attacks, do they? Well, neither did Christ, and neither should we. When we constantly pray and fast, we have "stockpiled faith" to draw from when great faith is needed. We are fully loaded and armed to the teeth for whatever sickness, obstacle, temptation, or trick the enemy launches at us.

Father, Give me the desire and the discipline to spend time in prayer and commit to fasting for the purpose of preparedness. Increase my faith so that no matter what I'm faced with, I have a stockpile of faith to draw from.

_____

_____

_____

_____

_____

_____

_____

_____

_____

_____

_____

_____

_____

_____

_____

_____

_____

_____

_____

_____

_____

NEVER RING THE BELL

But none of these things move me, neither count I my life dear unto myself, so that I might finish my course with joy, and the ministry, which I have received of the Lord Jesus, to testify the gospel of the grace of God. — ACTS 20:24, KJV

On the first day of Navy SEAL training, the primary instructor prepares the "tadpoles" for the grueling six-month course ahead of them. A large brass bell hangs in the asphalt courtyard, just a few feet away from the new trainees. After a terrifying description of the intense training, the instructor offers them an escape from the misery, "All you have to do to quit is ring this bell three times. Ring the bell and you won't have to get up early. Ring the bell and you won't have to do the long runs, the cold swims, or the obstacle course. Ring the bell and you can avoid all this pain." He also had another message: "If you quit, you will regret it for the rest of your life."[11] When Jon Sanchez went through SEAL training, 126 out of 140 men rang that bell. He did not. When asked what kept him going, he said, "I had a strong sense of purpose for being there."[12] Life is hard — grueling at times, and the enemy wants nothing more than to destroy your hope and rob you of your future. Don't let the struggles and sorrows of being human break you down. You have Holy Spirit power and a God-given purpose for being here. Persevere and cling to your purpose. You will regret it if you don't. Never give up. Never, ever ring the bell.

Lord, Keep my sights always on Your goal for me as I persevere, unwavering in my determination and discipline.

_____

_____

_____

_____

_____

_____

_____

_____

_____

_____

_____

_____

_____

_____

_____

_____

_____

_____

_____

_____

_____

One Last Thing Before I Go

I made known to them your name, and I will continue to make it known, that the love with which you have loved me may be in them, and I in them. -- John 17:26

Have you ever been alongside someone who had a terminal illness or been at the bedside of a loved one in their last days? There falls on them a sense of urgency to take care of business and express their most important thoughts while they can. When there is not much time, we easily separate out the unnecessary and focus on the indispensable. In the days before Gethsemane, in what is often called *The Last Prayer,* Jesus did the same. The Savior prayed for His disciples — all who would believe in Him for all of time — "that they may all be one, just as you, Father, are in me, and I in you," (John 17:20-21). Many teachings in the New Testament encourage the Church to live up to our purpose, demonstrating our love for Christ through connecting with one another. This is unity with a purpose greater than our individual fulfillment. As the crucifixion nears, this prayer explains why the Body's connection to the Father through the Son is on Jesus' heart. The second half of John 17:21 explains that we are called to be one "so that the world may believe that you [the Father] have sent me." Are you staying connected to other believers? Today, reach out to a few people to encourage them, and let them lift you in the process. In a world where so much attention is given to our differences and divisions, focus on what unites us.

Father, Keep me in Your love by Your power that I may draw the lost into a relationship with You. I will rely on Your Spirit for patience and kindness, not judging or gossiping, so the world will know I am Yours by my love.

KINDLE THEM WITH KINDNESS

But I say to you, Love your enemies and pray for those who persecute you, — MATTHEW 5:44

D o you know what a knee-jerk reaction is? I'm sure you do. It's a response that is automatic, rather than carefully thought out, and comes from the body's reflexes. When the doctor taps your knee with that little rubber hammer, your foot flies out automatically—a knee-jerk reaction. When someone is unkind or talks badly about you behind your back, without Fruit of the Spirit self-control, verbal flaming arrows can go flying from your mouth without a second of thought, damaging relationships, and reputations. But Jesus gave us the purest example of how we are to respond when someone tries to defame, bring shame, or discredit us: "When he was reviled, he did not revile in return; when he suffered, he did not threaten, but continued entrusting himself to him who judges justly" (1 Peter 2:23). If we bless those who hurt us, we leave their consequences and our comfort up to God. Free yourself from the anguish and grief of unforgiveness. If someone has hurt you, replaying it only keeps you in a cycle of pain. However, if by faith you "love your enemies, bless those who curse you, do good to those who hate you, and pray for those who spitefully use you and persecute you" (NKJV), hurt will be soothed and evil will be overcome with good.

Father, Give me strength to choose a common grace for all, just as You have, without distinction or denial to anyone, regardless of how I am treated. My love will not be based on how others are to me, but on who You are inside of me.

_____

_____

_____

_____

_____

_____

_____

_____

_____

_____

_____

_____

_____

_____

_____

_____

_____

_____

_____

_____

EL ROI

Why do you say, O Jacob, and speak, O Israel, "My way is hidden from the LORD, and my right is disregarded by my God?" — ISAIAH 40:27

In today's age of social media, video chats, and more than 200 streaming services in the US, we have the resources for expression like at no other time in history. We can reach and be reached by a limitless number of other humans, but still, many of us often feel unnoticed. Over half of employees feel "invisible" at work.[13] It is painful to be misunderstood and soul-crushing to feel unseen and unheard altogether. When we feel insignificant, forgotten, overwhelmed, and undervalued, we can remember that our Heavenly Father sees us. Our compassionate God is known for seeing those others refuse to acknowledge — the lepers, the demon-possessed, the outcast woman at the well — on and on, we see that no one escapes His sight or His love. When Abram and Sarai became so impatient for God's promise of a child to be fulfilled that Sarai sent her husband into the arms of their servant, Hagar, she became pregnant. Hagar produced exactly what the couple intended, and Sarai despised her for it. Of course, Hagar rubbed it in Sarai's face every chance she got. Eventually, Hagar fled with her son and ran into an angel who told her that she would have many descendants (Genesis 16). The despised and rejected mother of Ishmael knew that God saw her, though she had been undermined and underestimated by everyone around her. If you have ever felt invisible and, by extension, inadequate, believe me when I say that you are neither. No, do not believe *me*. Trust Your Creator. He is El Roi, *The God Who Sees.*

Lord, Thank You for Your faithfulness. I have made mistakes, but You have placed a treasure in me. Thank You for healing me, saving me, and dining with me. Thank You for seeing me, knowing me, and loving me.

_____
_____
_____
_____
_____
_____
_____
_____
_____
_____
_____
_____
_____
_____
_____
_____
_____
_____
_____
_____
_____
_____

POSTURE OF POWER

Before destruction a man's heart is haughty, but humility comes before honor. — PROVERBS 18:12

In the Sermon on the Mount, Jesus gave us what we call *The Beatitudes*, beginning with "Blessed are the poor in spirit, for theirs is the kingdom of heaven" (Matthew 5:3, NIV). Someone who is "poor in spirit" isn't lacking spirit; actually, they have the admirable quality of humility, realizing they have nothing to offer God but need His free gifts. Meekness is a similar characteristic. Matthew took notes on the mountainside, reporting Jesus also said that the meek are blessed and will inherit the earth. Being meek does not mean you are a doormat. Meekness is the positive character quality of dealing with people with kindness, humility, and consideration. People boast and brag, trying to prove themselves better than others — some to the point of sabotaging another person's success. They're like Veruca Salt from Willy Wonka & the Chocolate Factory: "I want it all, and *I want it now*!" Ms. Salt and those like her are confused. Loud and demonstrative people may seem strong, but they have no more power than a lightning bug could provide electricity to a city. Selfishness is not strength; pushy is not powerful. Pride demands respect, but humility will command it.

Father, I pray for a heart position of humility, not to cheapen my worth, but to align myself with a greater purpose than my own selfish gain. As I live in the freedom of meekness, help me to hold my value correctly, aware that I can do nothing without You.

Deliberate Defusal

When the Lord takes pleasure in anyone's way, he causes their enemies to make peace with them. — Proverbs 16:7

You don't have to be violent and loud to be destructive — silent treatment, passive-aggressive comments, or playing the victim can be just as detrimental to relationships as someone who expresses their agitation blatantly.

Special Agent Bomb Technicians are "specialized FBI officers whose job it is to identify, evaluate, and neutralize explosive devices."[14] Identifying each underlying cause or unhealthy thought pattern and disarming the lies. Differences in core values, ideas, and strategies combined with careless communication can fire up a minor offense until the whole thing blows up in your face, even among Christians.

The gospels reveal bits of the disciples' varied personalities, from the passionate Peter to the volatile "Sons of Thunder." Jesus' nickname for James and John seems to be a gentle reprimand to refine the young men. Luke 9:51-54 tells us the two were ready to call fire down on the heads of a couple of Samaritans who had insulted the Teacher. Instead of blessing the offenders and walking away, they wanted to burn the village to the ground! Jesus "rebuked them [and said, 'You do not know what kind of spirit you are of; for the Son of Man did not come to destroy men's lives, but to save them.'] And they went on to another village" (Luke 9:55–56, NASB). You can save your relationships and spare any hurt feelings by stopping disagreements at their core. Be gracious and forgiving, and remember what kind of Spirit *you* are of.

Father, Give me the compassion and patience to overlook an offense, the insight to see the true issues, and the steady hand and heart to calm any conflict so that others will see Your love in my responses.

_____

_____

_____

_____

_____

_____

_____

_____

_____

_____

_____

_____

_____

_____

_____

_____

_____

_____

_____

_____

_____

_____

WE ARE MANY, AND WE ARE ONE

Rather, speaking the truth in love, we are to grow up in every way into him who is the head, into Christ, from whom the whole body, joined and held together by every joint with which it is equipped, when each part is working properly, makes the body grow so that it builds itself up in love.
— EPHESIANS 4:15-16

In the Bible, the third chapter of Nehemiah begins the story of the rebuilding and repairing of the wall in Jerusalem. God gave Nehemiah the idea, so he inspected the structure and spoke with the authorities before getting the project started. God gave the vision to one man, but that man did not do the work alone. Chapter 3 records who did what, from who hung the doors to who built the Fish Gate. Just about everyone was involved – Goldsmiths, perfumers, governors' aids, merchants; the ruler of half the district of Jerusalem got his family involved, working side by side with his daughters in the baking district, constructing part of the western wall. Some had the skill and strength to repair a quarter of a mile stretch; others were only able to do smaller sections. Together, the members brought Nehemiah's vision to reality because they made it their own, and "the people worked with all their heart" (Nehemiah 4:6, NIV). This is what God expects from each of us. The work of the church's ministry belongs to everyone in the church. Are you owning the vision of the universal Church as well as your local fellowship? Select a portion of "the wall" and begin building and repairing, starting in your own home.

Father, I will not be a bystander, a spectator, in the church. This week, I commit to getting more involved in an area of ministry in the church, dedicating my family to the work of the Lord.

PRIDE AND DIE

The thief comes only to steal and kill and destroy. I came that
they may have life and have it abundantly. — JOHN 10:10

Early in the morning on August 29, 2005, Hurricane Katrina struck the Gulf Coast of the United States. The next day, Coast Guard Lieutenant Iain McConnell was ordered to fly his H46 helicopter around the clock to and from New Orleans in an effort to rescue those stranded by the storm. On their first three missions that day they saved eighty-nine people, three dogs, and two cats. On the fourth mission, Lt. McConnell and his brave crew saved no one. They flew twelve flights in that last mission, but not one person accepted their help. They asked for food and water to hold them over where they were — on rooftops or clinging to tree limbs. They were warned the waters would not be receding any time soon, but they refused to get in the helicopter.[15]

Jesus came to give life, abundant life. He came to save us, but still so many are fumbling around like there is no hope, barely surviving. Just scraping by spiritually is as excruciating as trying to have a good life with nothing but a few bites of bread and water. If you are clinging to the roof of an old, unhealthy way of life, refusing to cut ties to what once was or could have been, you are missing the abundant life God sent His Son to give you. Let go. Take the rescuer's hand and leave the wreckage behind for a better tomorrow.

My God, I admit my pride sometimes keeps me from accepting help. I have an idea of how things "should" be and it blinds me to the better blessing You have for me. Give me the humility to reach out and the vision to see more than my past. Thank You for this new life You have given me.

I Know the Way

Two people are better than one, because they can reap more benefit from their labor. For if they fall, one will help his companion up, but pity the person who falls down and has no one to help him up. — Ecclesiastes 4:9-10

If you were a fan of the political drama, *The West Wing* back in the early aughts, you may recall the episode after Deputy Chief of Staff Josh Lyman (Bradley Whitford) gets shot and is offered support from COS Leo McGarry (John Spencer). Leo, a war vet and recovering alcoholic, tells this story: "This guy's walking down the street when he falls down a hole. The walls are so steep he can't get out. A doctor passes by, and the guy shouts up, 'Hey, you! Can you help me out?' The doctor writes a prescription and throws it down in the hole and moves on. Then a priest comes along, and the guy shouts, 'Father, I'm down in this hole. Can you help me out?' The priest writes out a prayer, throws it down in the hole, and moves on. Then a friend walks by. 'Hey, Joe, it's me! Can you help me out?' And the friend jumps in the hole. Our guy says, 'Are you stupid? Now we're both down here.' The friend says, 'Yeah, but I've been down here before, and I know the way out.'"[16] Whichever character you may identify with in this parable, there is a powerful lesson here: God will send someone who's 'been there' to lead the way out of the pit. Maybe you are the mentor; perhaps you are the one needing some guidance. If you are the other passers-by, commit to doing more than offering powerless platitudes when someone is suffering. If you know the way, show the way.

Father, Thank You for using my experiences, pleasant and painful, to help others find their way. Help me to give beyond the minimum requirement and swallow my pride when I am the one who needs to ask for help.

_____

_____

_____

_____

_____

_____

_____

_____

_____

_____

_____

_____

_____

_____

_____

_____

_____

_____

_____

_____

How Much More

Or which one of you, if his son asks him for bread, will give him a stone? Or if he asks for a fish, will give him a serpent? If you then, who are evil, know how to give good gifts to your children, how much more will your Father who is in heaven give good things to those who ask him!
— Matthew 7:9-10

Many of Christ's parables began with "the Kingdom of God is like…" comparing it to something people of the time could relate to. Just like in the above verse, *The Parable of the Persistent Widow* in Luke 18 shows the contrast between what man will offer and what God desires to do for us when we pray and refuse to give up. Jesus said, "In a certain town there was a judge who neither feared God nor cared what people thought. And there was a widow in that town who kept coming to him with the plea, 'Grant me justice against my adversary.' For some time he refused. But finally he said to himself, 'Even though I don't fear God or care what people think, yet because this widow keeps bothering me, I will see that she gets justice, so that she won't eventually come and attack me'" (Luke 18:2-5, NIV)! Our God is no unjust judge who will keep putting us off, only giving in to get rid of us. He is just and will defend His chosen ones, not because of His frustration, but based on our faith. Be persistent, prove your faith, and your Father in Heaven will cover you — and how much more!

Thank You, my God, for loving me. All good things come from You. You have no human limitations to Your caring or Your patience. In faith, I will seek You and not give up!

_____
_____
_____
_____
_____
_____
_____
_____
_____
_____
_____
_____
_____
_____
_____
_____
_____
_____
_____
_____
_____
_____
_____

She Did Not Jump

and he died for all, that those who live might no longer live for themselves but for him who for their sake died and was raised. — 2 Corinthians 5:15

On Sunday, January 14, 1951, National Flight 83 from Newark to Norfolk was coming in for a layover in Philadelphia. Rain and snow had turned the runway to ice and slush causing the DC4 to crash through a fence at the end of the runway. A wing was severed, fuel tanks ruptured, and the plane ignited. A young woman named "Frankie" Housley was on that plane. She wrestled open the cabin door looking down to safety below. Passengers were screaming, children were crying, and smoke and flames were threatening an explosion, but she did not save herself. In a moment when survival instincts would have kicked in for most of us, Frankie chose to go toward the flames to help others. Working quickly to release people's seatbelts, she made nearly a dozen trips from the door to the main cabin, escorting people through the smoke to the doorway where they escaped death. Hours later, when the fire was put out, and the debris cooled, Frankie Housley's body was found wrapped around a 4-month-old baby she had tried to pull from the wreckage. She died so that others would be saved.[17]

Our Savior sacrificed His spot in Heaven, gave His time to train up the disciples, left behind a roadmap for us to follow, and accomplished His purpose on earth — dying so that you and I can live. Who are you willing to sacrifice for? How far will you go to pull a stranger from the fiery gates of Hell?

My God, Give me the courage and the character to put others first. Make me willing to sacrifice my comfort, my preferences and my plan to bring the gospel to those around me.

Count On It

So God has given both his promise and his oath. These two things are unchangeable because it is impossible for God to lie. Therefore, we who have fled to him for refuge can have great confidence as we hold to the hope that lies before us.
— Hebrews 6:18, NLT

When you sit in a chair, you expect it to hold you. When you flip the light switch, you don't even think about whether the lamp will turn on. For most of us, in the morning, we have the sun; at night, the moon is in the sky. There are some things we come to expect because of our experience. What do you put your trust in? Where do you turn? Who do you know that you know that you know you can count on? The second chapter of Timothy gives us a standard:

"Here is a trustworthy saying:

If we died with him,

we will also live with him;

if we endure,

we will also reign with him.

If we disown him,

he will also disown us;

if we are faithless,

he remains faithful,

for he cannot disown himself." — 2 Timothy 2:11-13

The Lord cannot act apart from His character. Count on it.

Father, I put my trust only in You. Keep my eyes open to how You are working in my life and remind me of all You have done and who You have been to me throughout the years...even when I didn't realize it.

_____

_____

_____

_____

_____

_____

_____

_____

_____

_____

_____

_____

_____

_____

_____

_____

_____

_____

_____

JESU JUVA

Commit everything you do to the LORD. Trust him, and he will help you. — PSALM 37:5, NLT

Suppose you're familiar with the German composer, Johann Sebastian Bach. In that case, you may know that at the bottom of his manuscripts, he wrote the initials, "S. D. G." for *Soli Deo Gloria* — "glory to God alone." Powerful words, committing his works to God and for His glory. What is just as meaningful is what he scribbled at the top of the page before one note had been scratched into the parchment: *Jesu Juva,* Latin for "Jesus, help!"[18] A cry for the Creator's help came before anything else for Bach, as it should be for each of us.

Blind Bartimaeus refused to be silent, calling out to Jesus even when people told him to be quiet (Mark 10:46-52). The woman with the issue of blood crawled on all fours, risking it all just to touch the Messiah (Mark 5:25-34). The Israelites called out to God because of their bondage, and He sent Moses to lead the way out of captivity (Exodus 3:9). Think now of the areas in which you need the Lord to intervene and allow "Jesus, help" and "Glory to God alone" be the bookends for every decision or endeavor. When you put your trust in Him, He will never put you to shame.

Heavenly Father, I need Your help. Sometimes those words are the only prayer I have. I trust in You and commit everything I do to Your glory.

_____

_____

_____

_____

_____

_____

_____

_____

_____

_____

_____

_____

_____

_____

_____

_____

_____

_____

_____

MAKE YOUR MOVE

Then they cried to the Lord in their trouble, and he saved them from their distress. He brought them out of darkness, the utter darkness, and broke away their chains.
— PSALM 107:13-14, NIV

Bartimaeus was blind and a beggar. He had no real options but to spread his cloak out next to the road, hoping to collect a few coins each day. One day he heard that Jesus was near where he sat, so he began calling out to Him. The crowd following Jesus told the beggar to quiet down, but he only shouted louder, "Son of David, have mercy on me!" When Jesus heard him, he called him over. Bartimaeus threw aside his coat, jumped up, and made his way to Jesus. When the Rabbi asked what he wanted, the blind man said, "I want to see!" Instantly the man could see, and he followed Jesus down the road (Mark 10:46-52). Notice that Bartimaeus didn't wait for someone to feel sorry for him and approach him. He made the first move to get what he knew he needed. The blind man shouted over the crowd even when they shushed him. And when Jesus called to him, he threw aside the cloak he once used to catch the coins tossed to him, showing that he knew he would no longer need it because he had faith that he was steps away from sight. If you want to see God respond to your need, call out to Jesus, do not let anything or anyone discourage you, lay aside your old identity with its limitations, and follow Him down the road.

Lord, Help me to acknowledge my need and to seek You with all of my heart. I will put aside my old identity and my backup plans, trusting that You will break my chains.

_____

_____

_____

_____

_____

_____

_____

_____

_____

_____

_____

_____

_____

_____

_____

_____

_____

_____

_____

_____

_____

State Your Identity

*You were taught, with regard to your former way of life, to
put off your old self, which is being corrupted by its deceitful
desires; to be made new in the attitude of your minds;
and to put on the new self, created to be like God in true
righteousness and holiness.* — Ephesians 4:22-24, NIV

Identity is significant to every single human being. Your
self-concept is based on your experiences, physical image,
thoughts, and how you tend to label yourself in various
situations. It's a perception you have of your image, abilities,
and uniqueness. When introduced to someone new, we tend
to say something akin to *Name, Rank, and Serial Number:*
"John James — I'm the owner of 'Masks R Us.'" How
do you identify yourself? By your career? Your family or
relationships? Hobbies or interests, or some other label? Who
would you be with those things stripped away? One of the
first things the military does to its enlistees is to strip away
anything that doesn't benefit the soldier's purpose before
building the soldier. Isn't that what God has called us to do?
The Apostle Paul said to "put to death what is earthly in you
[…] seeing that you have put off the old self with its practices
and have put on the new self, which is being renewed in
knowledge after the image of its creator" (Colossians 3:5,
9-10). And there it is: you were made in the image of your
Creator, God the Father, maker of Heaven and Earth. You
are a new creation and what identifies you must benefit your
purpose in the Kingdom.

My Creator, Above all else, I am Yours. Your child. Your handiwork. I was created by You and for You. Help me see myself as You see me and surrender to the putting-off/ putting-on process of being transformed by renewing my mind.

SELF-MANAGEMENT

Like a city whose walls are broken through
is a person who lacks self-control.
— PROVERBS 25:28, NIV

Self-management is your ability to regulate your behaviors, thoughts, and emotions in a productive way.[19] Self-management, similar to self-control, is the byproduct of a level of maturity that needs no outside motivators to choose what is right and reject what is wrong. A toddler may need a slap on the hand from time to time but will grow to realize on his own that forks don't go in the electrical socket. In the same way, young Christians who need the Word spoon-fed to them and a stronger mentor to guide them will transform and be motivated intrinsically and through the Holy Spirit. No outside force can sway us. In Proverbs 25:28, Solomon compares a person who lacks self-control to a city with a wall that has come tumbling down. When Joshua fought the battle of Jericho, and the walls fell, the enemy was without defense and quickly overtaken. If we cannot reign ourselves in, manage our choices, and control our behavior, we will be vulnerable to every sort of attack from the enemy. "Any physical enemy can exploit it, and any spiritual enemy will take advantage of it," but the fruit of the Spirit is self-control.

Lord God, Cause Your Word to come alive in me, transforming my mind and character as I mature in holiness. I will guard myself against the enemies of my mind through my choices and behavior, being directed by Your Spirit.

Do the Best You Can
for the Next Five Minutes

*Therefore do not be anxious about tomorrow, for tomorrow
will be anxious for itself. Sufficient for the day is its own
trouble.* — Matthew 6:34

Are you ever overwhelmed by your list of things to do? Fired up about future plans and then burnt out over what it's going to take to reach those goals? There is a lot of work between conception and completion, no doubt. Scholars believe Jesus and the disciples walked more than 3,000 miles during His ministry, but just like Jesus, you don't have to do it all in one day. Take a breath and break down the journey into manageable moments.

Green Beret candidates go through a grueling three-week selection process to determine if they meet the criteria for the Special Forces Qualification Course. Altogether, they are looking at two years of testing and training just to achieve the minimum level of proficiency to be considered deployable on a Special Forces "A" Team.[20]

To lessen the mental stress, candidates are taught to concentrate on tackling short periods or smaller tasks. Rather than worrying about the twelve-mile ruck march ahead, they focus on marching the best they can for five minutes. When time is up, they fix their goal on the next five minutes. If you find yourself overwhelmed at the magnitude of what your goal requires, this mental strength will help. If you are trying a new work-out regimen, have a huge school or work project, or are looking at enduring six months of rehab for an injury, focus on smaller goals within the goal. Do the best you can for the next five minutes, then repeat until you complete the course.

Lord God, Help me to manage my focus on the next right step, trusting and relying on Your strength, looking only as far ahead as my efforts will directly influence. I will not become anxious over things I cannot control, but will keep marching ahead the best I can in this moment.

Situational Awareness

If any of you lacks wisdom, let him ask God, who gives
generously to all without reproach, and it will be given him.
— James 1:5

*D*iscernment is defined as "the quality of being able
to grasp and comprehend what is obscure; an act of
perceiving something; a power to see what is not evident to
the average mind."[21] The definition also stresses accuracy, as
in "the ability to see the truth." Formal education is good;
reasoning and logic are helpful, so we seek to increase our
knowledge, but Spiritual Discernment cannot be obtained
that way. Have you ever been in a conversation and sensed
something significant beneath what was being said? More
than reading between the lines, it's as though the Holy Spirit
allows you a peek behind the curtain of the obvious and
reveals what God needs you to be aware of to accomplish
something in this person's life. Or in your own. Or both. Only
God can increase our wisdom, but it is our responsibility
to ask Him for it, like Solomon did when God offered him
anything in the world. Motivated by the weight of his duties
to his people, Solomon's request was powerful and simple.
You can find it in 1 Kings 3:9: "Give your servant therefore
an understanding mind to govern your people, that I may
discern between good and evil, for who is able to govern
this your great people?" Walking into any situation knowing
you are "on coms" with the Spirit of God Himself, hearing
directly from Him, will allow you to be of more significant
influence in service and prayer.

Holy God, Attune my ears to Your Spirit, making me aware of what is obscure so I may serve Your people and glorify Your Name. Prepare me for the unknown by pulling back the curtain on my surroundings and spiritual atmosphere.

MEANS TO AN END

Commit your work to the Lord,
and your plans will be established. — PROVERBS 16:3

What image will pop into your head if I tell you not to think of a beach ball? Right. A beach ball. Tell a bowler to keep his eye on the gutter, and what will happen? Gutterball. Exactly. Put your attention in the wrong place, and your life will end up somewhere you never intended. Intentionally fix your focus on whatever will help you achieve what the Lord has assigned you to. If you concentrate your thoughts on the obstacles and restrictions, then your direction will be determined by those distractions and disturbances. Instead of thinking in terms of limitations, focus on goals. Envision your end result and then pull back to identify the thoughts, ideas, and actions that will lead you there. Most of all, do not abandon the Lord's path in attempting to accomplish His purpose. God will never get you to the right thing the wrong way. He will not ask you to lie, cheat, and steal to get it done because He cannot abandon His holiness. When you are working your way toward success, focus only on what fits God's means to an end.

God, So many thoughts are running through my mind. Keep me from getting sidetracked and help me perceive Your direction, so I can be inspired with new ideas about where to go from here with this task. Thank you for refreshing my mind with your wisdom as I focus on the right things.

MENTALLY TOUGH

And let steadfastness have its full effect, that you may be perfect and complete, lacking in nothing. — JAMES 1:4

Do you know what separates the successful from the unsuccessful? Those who finish while others are in the aid tent on race day? The mentally drained from the dynamo? Mentally tough people are consistent. We choose consistency in our schedules, values, prayer lives, responses to trouble or offense, activities, church attendance, ministry service, relationships, and financial choices. These are the non-negotiables we have set as criteria for a disciplined, fulfilling home and work life. What are your non-negotiables in what you spend time doing? Who are you hanging out with? What do you allow to come into your ears and eyes through podcasts, radio, television, and movies? Those choices will also mold your consistency in your decisions and responses. When we create guidelines for ourselves based on Godly principles and relentlessly stick to them, no matter which way the wind blows, we will not be thrown off course. When the enemy comes at you with some shiny or sweet temptation, it won't even get your second look because it doesn't fit your criteria for what you will accept in your life. When your decisions are determined by your character — the new creation God has made you into through the blood of Christ, you will enjoy the fruit of the Spirit, self-control.

Heavenly Father, I desire to live my life based on Your values, so I can stay on track no matter my challenges to glorify You in all I do. Help me set and stick to my boundaries and focus on what's important.

PREEMPTIVE STRIKE

But stay awake at all times, praying that you may have strength to escape all these things that are going to take place, and to stand before the Son of Man. — LUKE 21:36

In his 1962 State of the Union Address, John F. Kennedy shared some wisdom: "The time to repair the roof is when the sun is shining." Have you ever known someone who seemed to always be running around *putting out fires?* Surely, some of our little fires couldn't have been predicted, but many happen due to a lack of preparedness. When you know the cold winter months are coming, do you find out your heater is busted when there's snow on the ground? Or do you test it when it's still warm outside? So often, we wait for an emergency to act when we could have avoided the catastrophe with a bit of prep. Noah didn't wait for the rain to start building the ark or gathering food (Genesis 6). Jesus didn't leave the demon-possessed boy to go off and fast and pray so He could heal him (Mark 9:29). If you want to stand any chance of taking down the enemy when he comes to "steal, kill, and destroy" your family, don't wait until there's an attack to prepare in prayer. Be pro-active. Execute a pre-emptive strike against the darkness before it has a chance to take over your home.

Holy God, protect my family and friends today. Keep them from harm and guide their steps. Send Your Holy Spirit ahead of them and surround them with Your angels. Give me the strength, wisdom, and discipline to keep our home protected in Your promise through prayer and preparedness.

_____
_____
_____
_____
_____
_____
_____
_____
_____
_____
_____
_____
_____
_____
_____
_____
_____
_____
_____
_____
_____

FORGIVENESS IS FREEDOM

Bearing with one another and, if one has a complaint against another, forgiving each other; as the Lord has forgiven you, so you also must forgive.
— COLOSSIANS 3:13, NASB

Perhaps you've heard this quote on forgiveness: "To forgive is to set a prisoner free and discover that the prisoner was you."[22]   Lewis B. Smedes, the author who penned that powerful revelation, also said, "Forgiving does not erase the bitter past. A healed memory is not a deleted memory. Instead, forgiving what we cannot forget creates a new way to remember. We change the memory of our past into a hope for our future."

Forgiving doesn't make you a punching bag. Forgiving is not the same as tolerating or condoning bad behavior. Many people withhold forgiveness because they feel that to forgive is to pretend there was no offense. That is not it at all. If someone has hurt you, you can acknowledge the misdeed and choose to not hold it against the person. It may take time for you to stop thinking of the offense each time you hear the person's name, still healing and reconciliation will come in stages. Some damage will take longer to repair. Forgiveness is intentional; healing is eventual. But if you are waiting for the memory to stop hurting before you forgive, you are doing it backward. Forgiving the person who hurt you will heal you and set you free.

Heavenly Father, Help me to forgive as You have forgiven me. You say to let all bitterness and anger be put away from me and to be kind and forgiving. Fill my heart with compassion so I can be gracious and righteous and free from bitterness.

_____

_____

_____

_____

_____

_____

_____

_____

_____

_____

_____

_____

_____

_____

_____

_____

_____

_____

_____

_____

_____

_____

It's in the Pages

All Scripture is breathed out by God and profitable for teaching, for reproof, for correction, and for training in righteousness, that the man of God may be complete, equipped for every good work. — 2 Timothy 3:16-17

WGRZ News in Buffalo, New York, reporting on the war in Iraq, told the story of 22-year-old Army Private First Class Brendan Schweigart who was on a critical mission. Before going out to battle, he tucked his bible in his pocket under his bulletproof shield. While on the mission, Schweigart was shot with a high-powered rifle but saved by his shield and the Sword of the Spirit. Brendan received a Purple Heart and was soon released from the hospital. When asked about the incident, his mother, Kim Scott, told reporters that her son loved God and always carried his Bible with him. Reporter Jessica Weinstein asked Ms. Scott if they still had the bullet that didn't make it to her son's heart that day and the soldier's mother replied, "Yes. It's in the pages." God's Word is our protection. In the darkest times, cover your heart with the Living Word of God, and the enemy's fiery darts cannot break through. Know the Word. Pray the Word. Praying the Scriptures out loud will nurture your faith, dispel the darkest depression and anxiety, and leave the devil no room to counter your attack. Jesus spoke the Word of the Father to the enemy in the wilderness, and the devil ran away, humiliated, and defeated. Keep God's Word in your heart, and you will prove again that your protection is in the pages.

Heavenly Father, Guard and transform my heart as I pray Your Word — Your will. Your living Word brings freedom, discernment, and protection. Cultivate in me a radical devotion to You through Your Holy Word.

_____

_____

_____

_____

_____

_____

_____

_____

_____

_____

_____

_____

_____

_____

_____

_____

_____

_____

_____

_____

WINNING THROUGH WORSHIP

But you are a chosen race, a royal priesthood, a holy nation, a people for his own possession, that you may proclaim the excellencies of him who called you out of darkness into his marvelous light. — 1 PETER 2:9

"We do not know what to do, but our eyes are on you, O LORD." This is the desperate cry of King Jehoshaphat after his scouts reported that three great armies were coming to attack his people. All of Judah stood before God until He spoke through a musician named Jahaziel. He said, "You will not need to fight in this battle. Stand firm, hold your position, and see the salvation of the Lord on your behalf." Everyone got up early the following day, Jehoshaphat selected the singers and marched them out to the front line. The worshippers went ahead of the warriors. The worship team belted out, "'Give thanks to the LORD, for his steadfast love endures forever.' And when they began to sing and praise, the Lord set an ambush against the men of Ammon, Moab, and Mount Seir, who had come against Judah, so that they were routed" (2 Chronicles 20:21-22). Judah showed up in time to see nothing but dead bodies lying on the ground. What challenges are ahead of you this week? What enemies are rising up against your family? God has given you victory. Move forward in worship, watch what God will do on your behalf, and collect your spoils!

Lord Father, You have brought me out of darkness and clothed me in the light of Your complete love. You set me free, provide for me and protect me. I trust in You. When I do not know what to do, my eyes will stay on You.

DEFENSIVE MANEUVERS

Do not enter the path of the wicked, and do not walk in the way of the evil.
Avoid it; do not go on it; turn away from it and pass on.
— PROVERBS 4:15-16

There is a lot that goes into boxing at exclusive levels. As any trainer will tell you, fighting is not all fire and fury, but footwork. The creator of the Ali Shuffle, Muhammad Ali, would "float like a butterfly, and sting like a bee." The ability to dance and dodge the opponent's jabs, glide and gain an advantageous position gives a boxer ring generalship, controlling the ring's atmosphere and making him harder to hit. In this world, you can expect evil (1 Peter 4:12), but you can also escape it (Matthew 6:13). How is your footwork? What is your positioning? If you allow ungodly influences to breathe in your face, you are up close and personal with the things of this world and will be easy to knock out. But "flee from sexual immorality" (1 Corinthians 6:18), "abstain from the passions of the flesh, which wage war against your soul" (1 Peter 2:11), and "guard the deposit entrusted to you." (1 Timothy 6:20). If you find yourself in a pattern of gossip, overeating, *going too far* in a relationship or just in your imagination, do not let yourself get comfortable there. As two-time featherweight national champion Willie Pep said, "If you hit and run away, you live to fight another day."

Dear God, Show me where I am inviting temptation into my life. I don't want to make bad decisions that give the enemy a foothold in my life. When You show me the way of escape, I will take it.

_____

_____

_____

_____

_____

_____

_____

_____

_____

_____

_____

_____

_____

_____

_____

_____

_____

_____

_____

_____

_____

_____

_____

VETERANS OF SPIRITUAL WARS

You therefore must endure hardship as a good soldier of Jesus Christ. No one engaged in warfare entangles himself with the affairs of this life, that he may please him who enlisted him as a soldier. — 2 TIMOTHY 2:3-4 NKJV

S aul enlisted into the Lord's army on the road to Damascus. The encounter with God left him physically blind but gave him spiritual sight, changing his mission and name (Acts 9). In his letter to Timothy, Paul outlines the requirements of a good soldier:

Enlist: God does not use a forced draft to get us to follow Him. We join up, fully devoted to His leadership for whatever He requires and desires. And we never regret it. Even in the hard times.

Endure: Paul was no stranger to hardship but embraced his suffering. James said it clearly: "Consider it all joy, my brothers *and sisters*, when you encounter various trials, knowing that the testing of your faith produces endurance" (James 1:2-3, NASB).

Engage: We must be actively involved in the "tearing down of strongholds" and "taking captive" the thoughts that come against our objective. We do not get ourselves entangled in trivialities and foolishness but are intentional about the paths we take and the choices we make.

If you have chosen to follow Christ, do not get tangled up in the issues and distractions around you. Keep your focus, endure the stresses, and actively engage in the things that bring honor to the Lord.

Lord God, I commit to being a good soldier, engaging in each mission, willing to endure trials to see Your purpose come to life through me.

_____
_____
_____
_____
_____
_____
_____
_____
_____
_____
_____
_____
_____
_____
_____
_____
_____
_____
_____
_____
_____
_____

First Thing's Last

Who is to condemn? Christ Jesus is the one who died—more than that, who was raised—who is at the right hand of God, who indeed is interceding for us. Who shall separate us from the love of Christ? — Romans 8:34-35

Are you having a good week? Are you making wise choices? Have you honored God in every single choice, each situation? No matter how you answere, do you believe your behavior can heighten or hinder your Father's love for you? God's love does not ebb and flow. Your choices affect your character but do not affect the Lord's. He is unchanging and that's great news for sinners (ie all of us). David was a man after God's own heart. Even after he peeped at Bathsheba in the tub, slept with her, tried to cover it up, and murdered her husband? *Yes. Even then.* Psalm 51 is the cry of David's heart, his suffering and guilt for what he had done, his repentance, and his assurance of God's steadfast love. After the Prophet Nathan delivered the message of God's judgement to David, he suffered severe consequences, none of them the loss of God's love. The love of the Father remained steady and sure and undeniable even after David's horrible choices. What mistakes have you made? God loves you even when you fail. That confidence is not a license to sin but a cause for surrender and obedience. When you mess up — and you will, thank God for His Son, who died so that you can remain in good standing with the Father. And pray this prayer of David:

Be gracious to me, God, according to Your faithfulness;

According to the greatness of Your compassion, wipe out my wrongdoings.

Wash me thoroughly from my guilt And cleanse me from my sin.

[...] Create in me a clean heart, God, And renew a steadfast spirit within me.

Do not cast me away from Your presence, And do not take Your Holy Spirit from me.

Restore to me the joy of Your salvation, And sustain me with a willing spirit. Then I will teach wrongdoers Your ways, And sinners will be converted to You.

— PSALM 51:1-2, 10-13, NASB

ENDNOTES

1   Coelho, Paulo, and M. Dolors Ventós. Brida. Labutxaca, 2016.

2   Ruskin, John. The Stones of Venice Vol. 1. Vol. 1, Dent, 1907.

3   Wire, CNN. "'Float like a Butterfly, Sting like a Bee': Best Quotes from Muhammad Ali." KTLA, KTLA, 4 June 2016, https://ktla.com/news/nation-world/float-like-a-butterfly-sting-like-a-bee-best-quotes-from-muhammad-ali/?msclkid=2eef5b4fcfb411ec8a68f57feb64113c.

4   Clark-Sheard, Karen, and Richard Smallwood. "Secret Place." The Ultimate Collection, Word/Warner/Curb.

5   Lounsbrough, Craig D. A View from the Front Porch: Encounters with Life and Jesus. Revival Nation Publishing, 2009.

6   "Walking in Wisdom." Ligonier Ministries, 8 Aug. 2010, https://www.ligonier.org/posts/walking-wisdom.

7   "Albert Einstein Quote: 'Knowledge Is Realizing That the Street Is One Way; Wisdom Is Looking in Both Directions Anyway.'" Quotefancy, https://quotefancy.com/quote/763474/.

8   consistency. (n.d.) Random House Kernerman Webster's College Dictionary. (2010). Retrieved October 21 2022 from https://www.thefreedictionary.com/consistency

9   Nicholson, Robert. "Opinion | A Coronavirus Great Awakening?" The Wall Street Journal, Dow Jones & Company, 26 Mar. 2020, https://www.wsj.com/articles/a-coronavirus-great-awakening-11585262324.

10   Hoelscher, Jeff. "September 2 Is the 75th Anniversary of End of World War II." VA News, 2 Sept. 2020, https://news.va.gov/78513/september-2-75th-anniversary-end-world-war-ii/#:~:text=September%202%20 is%20the%2075th%20anniversary%20of%20end,dinner%20and%20told%20 them%20the%20war%20was%20over.

11   Archino, Joe. "Never, Ever, Ring the Bell! Life Lessons from a Navy Seal." Thisiswhywestand, 16 Aug. 2018, https://www.thisiswhywestand.net/single-post/2018/08/15/Never-Ever-Ring-the-Bell-Life-Lessons-From-a-Navy-Seal.

12   Sanchez, Jon. "Never Ring the Bell." Team Performance Institute, 9 Aug. 2017, https://teamperformanceinstitute.com/never-ring-the-bell/.

13   "2018 Global Culture Report." O.C. Tanner - Appreciate Great Work, 14 Sept. 2018, https://www.octanner.com/global-culture-report.html.

14   "FBI Bomb Technician Program Jobs and Salary." How to Become an FBI Agent | FBI Requirements, Wiley University Services, 2 Apr. 2021, https://www.fbiagentedu.org.

15   "People in New Orleans Refuse to Be Rescued by Helicopter." Family Times, 2022, https://www.family-times.net/illustration/Warning/202403/.

16   Kleine, Andrew. "Lead like Leo: Lessons from 'the West Wing." Government Executive, Government Executive, 14 Apr. 2021, https://www.govexec.com/management/2020/12/lead-leo-lessons-west-wing/170598/.

17   "Opinion | the Heroic Story of Frankie Housley, Flight Attendant." The Wall Street Journal, Dow Jones & Company, 3 May 2022, https://www.wsj.com/articles/airplane-crash-landin-housley-flight-attendant-steward-ess-11651521871.

18   Bangert, Mark. "Johann Sebastian Bach on the Christian Life." Evangelical Lutheran Church in America, 1 May 2010, https://www.elca.org/JLE/Articles/308.

19   Raeburn, Alicia. "What Is Self-Management? (7 Skills to Improve It) • Asana." Asana, 3 May 2022, https://asana.com/resources/self-management.

20   Chace, , Dave. "Special Forces Soldiers Graduate Qualification Training; Honor Green Beret with Soldier's Medal." Www.army.mil, SWCS Public Affairs Office, 18 May 2012, https://www.army.mil/article/80133/special_forces_soldiers_graduate_qualification_training_honor_green_beret_with_soldiers_medal.

21   GotQuestions.org. "How Can I Increase My Spiritual Discernment?" GotQuestions.org, 4 Jan. 2022, https://www.gotquestions.org/spiritual-discernment.html.

22   Smedes, Lewis B. Forgive and Forget: Healing the Hurts We Don't Deserve. HarperSanFrancisco, 2007.

About The Author

Jamaal Bernard is a cultural strategist and innovator for his generation. As the COO of Christian Cultural Center, his vision is to lead strong without compromising compassion.

Along with this role, he also has the privilege of serving as the Senior Pastor at Christian Cultural Center's Long Island Campus. As an extension of CCC in Brooklyn, Jamaal was able to watch his father, Reverend A.R. Bernard, build the storefront ministry into New York City's largest church, with a registered membership of over 37,000.

Jamaal Bernard is leading a movement of Unapologetic Ambassadors for Christ (UAFC), a clarion call to be unwilling to apologize for your faith and beliefs. Bernard's previous book, *Unapologetic Christianity*, is a critical tool that advances the gospel by equipping its readers with practical answers to questions about their faith. Jamaal Bernard is passionate about sharing the love of Jesus in every realm of his life and ministry.

Jamaal and Rita, his wife of more than twenty years enjoy working together in ministry. They have five children: Kamryn, Stephanie, Jamall Jr., Liam, and Maali.

Lightning Source UK Ltd.
Milton Keynes UK
UKHW050157240223
417504UK00017B/1152